The Forgiveness Effect

A Journey of Courage, Hope, Healing and Freedom!

by Lou Samara

Personality
INSIGHTS
PRESS

Editor – Nancy J. Marbry
Cover design, and layout – Pedro A. Gonzalez

Published by:
Personality Insights, Inc.
P.O. Box 28592, Atlanta, GA 30358-0592
1-770-509-7113

www.personalityinsights.com

ISBN: 978-1-7329364-1-6
First Edition: February 2019

PRINTED IN THE UNITED STATES OF AMERICA

TABLE OF CONTENTS

How easy it is to blame our problems on others. "Look at what he's doing..." "Look how long I've waited..." "Why doesn't she call...?" "If only he'd changed then I'd be happy..."

*Often, our accusations are justified. We probably are feeling hurt and frustrated. In those moments, we may begin to believe that the solution to our pain and frustration is getting the other person to do what we want or having the outcome we desire. But self-defeating illusions put the power and control out of life in other people's hands. We call this **codependency**.*

*The solution to our pain and frustration, however valid, is to acknowledge our own feelings. We feel the anger, the grief; then we let go of the feelings and find peace - within ourselves. We know our happiness isn't controlled by another person, even though we may have convinced ourselves it is. We called this **acceptance**.*

*Then we decide that although we'd like our situation to be different, maybe our life is happening this way for a reason. Maybe there is a higher purpose and plan in play, one that's better than we could have orchestrated. We call this **faith**.*

*Then we decide what we need to do, what is within our power to do to take care of ourselves. That's called **recovery**.*

It's easy to point our finger at another, but it's more rewarding to gently point it at ourselves.

The Language of Letting Go *(Daily Meditations, October 11th)*
- Melody Beattie

FOREWORD

About 20 years ago I got up one morning and went to the gym for an early morning work-out. I was staying in a hotel in Jacksonville, Florida, speaking at a convention. Little did I know I was about to have an "important encounter". While I was working out that morning, I met another gentleman in the hotel gym by the name of Lou Samara. We sort of helped each other out with the weights during our morning work-out program. After we finished, we struck up a conversation about business and life in general. We were both amazed at how many views we held in common. The conversation led to further interactions over the coming days and weeks and months. I soon realized I had met a new friend.

Over the years, we have had many opportunities to interact with one another. We have both been through some challenging experiences in life. We have been able to coach one another and encourage each other through the good times as well as the more difficult ones. Who would have thought that simply going to the gym could produce such lifelong results!

In this book, Lou has poured out his heart and life to help give the reader guidance and encouragement for daily living. None of us gets to choose the events that come our way, but we all get to choose how we respond to them. Someone once wisely noted that life is about 10% what happens to you and 90% how you respond to it! That is why I like Lou Samara as well as this excellent book he has written; it helps us on this journey called life!

This book is not theory, it is experience! The way we deal with the events of life is up to each one of us. However, it is important that we have guidance along the way from someone older or wiser than ourselves to help show us how to walk the path of life in such a manner as to bring about good results. That is what this book is.

Respectfully,
Robert A. Rohm, Ph.D.
President, Personality Insights, Inc.
Atlanta, GA

TESTIMONIALS

"I am thrilled that you are reading The Forgiveness Effect by my friend, Lou Samara. We have all seen successful people, but what we do not often see are people who are real and successful. That is Lou and this book proves it. In a world where very, few high achievers let down their guards, Lou lets you into his life. And then he beautifully steps into yours with his book, offering hope and answers for some of humanity's biggest challenges. Winners are winners in life and business. Lou is both and The Forgiveness Effect will help you to become a winner too."

R.D. SAUNDERS | R.D. Saunders

Vice President of Advancement

John Maxwell's EQUIP Leadership Organization

https://maxwellcenter.com/

"Lou's captivating and challenging journey is an inspiration for all of us; we all can easily become the victim, or we can become the champion of our own destiny. The Forgiveness Effect demonstrates how each decision we make, molds the outcome of our future. I would recommend this book no matter the adversity small or large, we might be facing; as it provides hope, inspiration and determination for all of us to never forget that we have within ourselves to overcome and live the life God has planned for us".

Kevin E. France
Founder – Managing Partner
Momentum Consulting Group, Inc.
www.MomentumConsultingGrp.com

INTRODUCTION

In an old movie, the doctor might say, "You don't remember it because you're blocking it out." He's partially correct because *you are* not blocking anything out. Your mind records everything. Your mind, however, chooses not to store some memories in your conscious memory to protect you!

The brain works in mysterious ways. This book is not about how the blocking happens, please simply trust that it does. Instead, it's about the aftermath of that memory suppression and what happens when we suppress hurtful events along with the emotions attached to those events. Once we are open to those memories, we need to learn how to process the emotions associated with them to heal. So, we can get free from our past hurts.

My mind shut out some truly horrific events that happened to me as I was growing up. Although the memories were buried deep in my subconscious, well into adulthood, the mental 'programming' from those events contributed greatly to my 'downfall'. These events spurred me on to turn my life around, to heal, to live a life of abundance and gratitude. I went from the depths of despair and darkness to awareness and, reluctantly at first, to acceptance. Then it was all about letting go, which comes from being able to truly love … and to forgive.

This book is about my story, my personal journey to a new and better life! I hope you see so much more.

It's about how we can *all* work through our mental and physical suffering, fears, self-doubt—the list could go on—and find our *true* selves, experience real love and thus discover the levels of peace and happiness that we never thought possible.

Although the lessons learned, and healing processes were often challenging, painful and took many years, I am extremely *grateful* for all those experiences. That may seem hard to believe, but it is true. Those events have become some of the greatest gifts in my life. I have experienced considerable growth and I now have a richness in my life that I never dreamed possible.

My relationships are healthy and strong; I married my dream girl Leslie, and my son Louis and I have a flourishing relationship. I've built a highly successful, sustainable company and am now starting on my next venture. I am continually creating my life, one that before the described events, I could only dream of.

You too, can overcome and heal if you choose to forgive those who have mentally or physically hurt you throughout the course of your life. You see, forgiveness won't change the past; it will, however, change your future. It's what I call *The Forgiveness Effect.*

To your health and happiness,

Lou Samara

For a Free Offer go to: www.forgivenesseffect.com/freeoffer

DEDICATION

It's most unfortunate—and I truly wish it were different—but I know that I am far from alone in being abused. Quite simply, this book is dedicated to all my fellow sufferers.

In every way I can be, I am 'with you' on your journey because I have experienced this too. Know this: You can, no you will, overcome where you are today if you decide to accept where you are, learn to trust, let go and forgive, while moving forward with your life. To do this, you must accept that there is help and relief available if you seek it out—you just need to start looking. I have made doing that as easy as I can for you.

There are some excellent approaches, therapies, life skills that can help the conscious and unconscious memory systems pool their information and work together for our well-being. I have mentioned numerous resources throughout the book, and these are also summarized at the end to help you with this process. Also, you can find even more details on my website at www.forgivenesseffect.com

Whatever your reason for reading this book, I thank you from the bottom of my heart. I pray that you can have the opportunity to become emotionally free, will learn how to forgive and let go so you—and your transgressors—can live full, happy, healthy, and productive lives.

ACKNOWLEDGMENTS

There are so many people to thank here; I could fill another book with their names. If you know me personally, then *you* are included in this most important list because I value our relationship. However, there are those I must mention specifically, and I offer my gratitude to:

The Good Lord who saw to it that I would be set free from the horrible memories and ties that bound me to a life of unhealthy ignorance.

My beautiful wife Leslie, who has been able to change her life mid-stream to learn how to live the life of an entrepreneur and to accept that no matter how perfect life seems, everyone has been challenged in some way. I am grateful she has accepted me over my past and loves me for the man I am now and still becoming.

My son Louis, who, although he may not fully understand everything that has happened, has been a wonderful source of joy and love in my life. He is a terrific young role model with a brilliant future, and I am so very proud to be his dad.

My mom, who taught me how to be a good citizen, friend, son, and father. She gave me the basis for my life, protected and guided me to make sure I grew up with a strong sense of faith and family and continues to be a source of invaluable support in my life.

My dad, who like my mom, loved and encouraged me as well as, guided me when I needed it most. He was always on my side even when it seemed like life was against me. Although he left this life prematurely many years ago, his memory continues to be a positive influence.

Rachel, who will always be a very important person in my life. Her patience, non-judgement and loving support have been a guiding light. She has been a steady advocate to help me work through my issues and a consistent reminder to treat myself well, to be myself... and that we are never done growing!

Brad who, for over twenty years, has been a mentor helping me through many rough spots. Now, as friends, we continue to support each other through life.

Charles, without whom I may never have had the opportunity to get free. His tough love was instrumental in helping me accept what happened and without that, I would have never been able to grow in my faith and relationships.

Tim, who has been one of the best friends a person could have! His intuitive questions and patience have helped me grow in many areas of my life.

All my coaches, advisors and mentors who have patiently encouraged, advised and helped me on my journey.

Wendy who has been my personal trainer and confidant for over 11 years. Her non-judgment and patience while listening to my challenges have greatly helped me move through my process.

John my close cousin who for many years supported and listened to me while taking me for many enjoyable dinners! We continue to be close allies through life!

Graham, my writer and editor, without whom this book would still be in pieces! It's thanks to him you are reading this!

Nancy, my editor, spent countless hours reading and re-reading and reviewing! She is another reason you have this book.

My former wife, although we are no longer married, she gave me a wonderful son and encouraged him to pursue his dreams. Thank you for your forgiveness, please know that you too are forgiven!

Darkness cannot drive out darkness;
only light can do that.
Hate cannot drive out hate;
only love can do that.

- Martin Luther King, Jr.

"The weak can never forgive. Forgiveness is the
attribute of the strong."

- Mahatma Gandhi

PROLOGUE

For the first time in ages, I felt excited about something. It was the Friday prior to Thanksgiving week, November 2003. I had received a call from my boss. He said he wanted to meet me, at my office, Monday morning to talk about 'growing my region'. Finally, I thought, after three years of uphill battles with him, I was getting my chance to show what I could do. Our company was recently acquired by a global public corporation. I thought maybe the new company was going to give me the opportunity to grow and develop my region.

As far as I was concerned, this was *the* reason I was hired, but it seemed like I was being held back since joining the company in 2000. In all that time, I had been itching to get a chance to grow the business. No wonder I was so elated!

All that weekend, I was jotting my ideas down in my notebook and constantly thinking about what changes could be made to improve the business. When Monday morning finally arrived, I was more than prepared. The corporate headquarters was in Delaware, but my boss was coming to meet with me at my office in New Jersey. I arrived early, made sure the office was clean and organized. I sat excitedly waiting, running through all the ideas I wanted to discuss during the meeting.

Somewhat later than expected, I heard the knock on my door, when I answered, I saw his new boss with him. This was an unannounced surprise. Instantly my heart sank; somehow, I knew this wasn't good news. I asked if I could get them some coffee or water, but they refused. This was another bad sign! Now the feelings of worry started to overwhelm me. My mind started racing with questions. Why was this other guy here? Why, had he lied about the purpose of the meeting?

After a few minutes of polite, but artificial conversation, he got to the *real* reason for seeing me when he mentioned the name of another firm in our industry. A while ago I had done a job for them on my own time—they were not competitors—but I had not told my boss about it. When the matter came to the surface, it was a big issue for him to say the least, he wasn't happy. I tried to explain that there was no conflict of interest or detriment to our company, but he didn't care to discuss it. The more I justified my actions, the less secure I felt! It was horrible. I felt like I was being accused of some heinous crime, all the while forgetting I was free to do what I chose to do with my off time.

"We are letting you go."

The words no one ever wants to hear. So many thoughts were running through my head, I was married with a 6-year-old son, a mortgage, car payment, and too many other bills to count. Then there was the fact that it was the Monday of Thanksgiving week. Perfect timing!

"I'll pay you the money I earned on that job, how about that?" I said.

Even before the words left my mouth, I knew it was a desperate and pitiful thing to say, but I was panicking and felt frightened. As the true reason for the meeting began to sink in, I started thinking of how I would break the news to my wife. Our relationship was already strained, and this would increase the level of stress at home.

Getting fired was the culmination of a long list of stifling, hurtful, and oppressive experiences. This unexpected event, for the most trivial of reasons, was the one that shook me into finally accepting the fact that my life was just a mess! I knew that I had to do something about it. What I didn't—couldn't—know at the time, were the consequences of that decision. I had no idea what opening those new and different doors might reveal or the amazing impact that new understanding would have on my life.

together discussing business ideas, people, and positions. We also met with the Senior Vice President, Human Resources, with whom I also built a quick rapport. At the end of the day, the President even took me out for dinner. I was really touched and genuinely appreciated the time with him.

I was starting to get excited about my life again and at the prospect of doing better, feeling like I was moving upwards. The President said they would look to find a new position for me, but as of now, there was nothing open. Time dragged on. What was wrong with me? I even told my wife that things were looking up, so when my plans failed to materialize, it caused even more stress at home as well as at my job. Then, despite my learning from the 'University of Life', my lack of a bachelor's degree didn't sit well in this company's culture. They liked my ideas and me, but I didn't have the required levels of formal education. How on earth could that matter in this situation?

After a few months of calling back and forth, they still had no position for me … then they started to implement the strategies I recommended without giving me credit. I thought they liked me, but to not give me credit for my ideas? Now I felt used and angry that they would act like this after we had such good interactions. Maybe they weren't such gentlemen after all.

Another door had been slammed in my face, and I was desperate to get out and move up. I forced myself to start looking for some positives. I asked myself about my relationships and how I interacted with people. I was looking to grow in my career and felt I was stuck in my current position. I started circulating my resume and looking for ways to improve my skills. I came across a company that helped people 'groom' themselves for better success.

They took me through a mock interview process and critiqued my skills and determined I needed to improve my interview techniques. They offered an eight-week package to work alongside and coach me through the entire process of redesigning my resume, improving my interview skills and providing me with contacts in my industry to help secure a new position. The cost was $6,000. I put it on my Amex, which understandably caused more stress at home.

I didn't get much for my money. They walked a very small group of us through some interview questions once a week for eight weeks. Then they gave me a list of 100 names and addresses that I could send my resume to and wished me luck. I did as they suggested, and only received one or two calls and no interviews.

With the additional burden on my finances as well as my marriage, I felt desperate and trapped and couldn't think of a way out. I wondered if I could feel any worse about myself. My thinking was, "Why do people take advantage of me so easily? Am I just an easy target?"

2

More than 18 months had now gone by since things began to fall apart after the move to New Jersey. At home, the bills were mounting and even though I earned extra money from being part of the Amway business, the tension in my marriage was so constricting it felt like an overinflated balloon that could explode at any time. It looked like nothing was going to improve. Then one day, I was in a client's lab calibrating some equipment when I met a guy who said his company was looking for someone to perform service and calibration and asked if I knew anyone. I said, "Yeah, me!" He gave me his card and asked me to send a resume.

Working towards alleviating the negative things going on in my life, I learned a lot of skills by following one of Amway's affiliated personal development systems and building an Amway business. Working with a team of people after work hours and when I could on weekends, I had developed a business that grew to a level where I was nationally recognized. Since this was my only real career focused accomplishment in recent years, I put it on my resume. Once the COO of this potential new employer saw it, he immediately wanted to talk to me.

I went to see him to discuss the position. During the conversation, I shared my business growth ideas for a company like his in the pharmaceutical industry; he really liked them. He told me that he had been a part of the Amway business and knew that to get to the level I reached took a lot of work, dedication and good people skills, as well as integrity. After all my failures, he was as good as his word and I finally got a new job in 2000.

Despite the extra income from Amway, we were in danger of losing the house we committed to when we moved back to New Jersey. By implementing some of the new beliefs and strategies I learned from the development system of our Amway business, this new role saved us! I doubled my salary! This was huge for me. With almost an acre of land, our three-bedroom home was in a very nice, established neighborhood, situated in a solid upper middle-class town—I finally felt like I met that criteria. I asked myself, "Could I now be happy?"

To some extent and for a short while, the tension levels dropped at home. The major income boost, along with a promotion and better working environment, were all very helpful. My confidence was boosted for a while, but that feeling did not last very long. Once again, I had problems with my new boss who was a VP and had a ten percent ownership stake in the company. I would often think to myself, "Is it me? Am I unlucky? Is corporate America not a good fit for me or am I being pushed to grow for something else?" There seemed to be too many unanswered questions bouncing around below the surface!

I had always enjoyed meeting and speaking with the COO. My, soon to be, new boss and I never really clicked during the interview process. It seemed that the meetings and conversations that I had with the COO caused an immediate rift between my new boss and me. He seemed cynical about everything we talked about and he had a very strange way of going about our work.

I worked in a technically oriented industry, where many employees were highly analytical, which lead to a tendency of being skeptical. Additionally, people in New Jersey seemed to be a bit more high-strung and that spilled over into my home life. I worked hard to focus on staying positive because I knew how stress affected me. Many people in these positions were hired to fix equipment but lacked people and sales skills. At this time in my life, I felt so emotionally spent and feared that I lacked the competence to work in this arena because I took everything too personally.

When on our way to make a sales calls, my boss would ask if I was "ready to do battle" or when we were going out to meet potential clients to acquire their equipment service contracts, he would ask if I was "ready to go to war". I usually felt that he didn't want me there! I learned the hard way that his attitude was vastly different with other people. I soon became his #1 target. Why was I such a favorite for bullies?

One day my boss and I were sitting in his office, he said, "The COO told me all about your work ethic and your ... so called integrity, he wants you on the team. You, however, are on my team and that means doing things my way ..."

He left the sentence hanging, so I simply nodded.

"I will be the judge of your work ethic since it will relate to the work, I tell ... ask you to do!"

I said, "The COO said he wanted me to work on growing the company so ..."

"You're here as service manager, so you'll do just that—servicing. Growing the company is up to me and you're not able to do that. I presume I've made myself clear?"

All I could do was nod my head again, but already the extra money was meaning very little and my newfound confidence was draining fast. I spoke to the COO about it, but he just told me to speak directly with my boss. I wanted to ask him to do that for me, but he just shrugged me off with a shake of his hand saying that I knew why he hired me. Yes, I did, but the VP was stopping me from doing it!

So, I carried on with my job and tried to settle in, while things at home with my wife were better. At times, I could even feel more of my natural outgoing self, more like when I had been a cop in Colorado. Back then I was tough and strong. Perhaps more of a 'go-getter' than some, but I always looked to do more than just showing up and do my job as described on paper, like some obedient servant. But now that's all I was expected to do, just show up and do the minimum. While I tried to be like that, it was not me and I found it to be emotionally draining.

I talked to my team and encouraged them to try new ideas, but I didn't get very far. I thought my boss intimidated them, but he later told me that I was the one who intimidated people. I really didn't understand then realized, with some outside coaching help, that despite his ownership position, he saw me as a threat. We had a different interpretation of what the work ethic should be. He didn't know me nor I him. He didn't care to understand me and at that time, I didn't know how to understand him. After having more conversations with the COO and several other management personnel, I was told to try to work things out with my boss. Which I did but got nowhere.

I was on the road quite a bit for this job and had gotten into a habit of calling people, mostly family and friends in Colorado on my company cell phone I didn't realize I was using the phone so much. This caused another issue. Instead of my boss calling me into his office or speaking with me on the phone, he had a very different way of dealing with the issue.

"Next agenda item - cell phones," he announced at the monthly staff meeting, attended by my peers and team members. As he displayed an excel spreadsheet with the employee's cell phone usage, he said, "Some of you have been using these too much for personal calls—like the worst is over 3,000 minutes, and that's you, Lou—so you need to cut it out!" My peers mocked me.

Of course, I was wrong, but just like that, he embarrassed me in front of everyone. Because of my emotionally fragile state, it impacted me greatly. Now everyone around me seemed to see only my faults. I was feeling more and more like a failure. Sure, I deserved to be reprimanded, wouldn't it have been much more effective if it had been done on a one to one basis? I would have agreed to change my behavior; the matter would have been forgotten yet help me improve. Instead, it seemed to have been another huge blow to my self-esteem. At that point, I felt like I had committed some huge unethical crime.

As a manager, I was responsible for the performance of my team. On one project, I caught one of my team members stealing from a customer. After confronting him, I went directly to HR with the matter. However, I was the one who got in trouble! I was told I did not follow the 'chain of command' and tell my VP first. The guy got away with it by simply saying that he "needed the things". I, however, was reprimanded and a written warning was placed in my personnel file. Things were rapidly moving in a downward spiral at work and it was pretty much the same at home.

The tension in the air at home felt stifling! There wasn't any fighting, just a feeling of uneasiness. With all the work issues I was experiencing the pressure and anxiety I felt increased.

It seemed like every time I was at work my VP would raise another issue. This time was about my leadership skills.

Maybe I wasn't very good at 'leading' because I was more about directing and delegating as I had been when I was a police officer, yet I thought the guys on my team were happy with how we interacted. We would talk and seem to get along. I even got to know them personally, but then an issue was raised that I wasn't there enough for them. This was not about helping them solve problems but was simply the fact that I was the manager and had other responsibilities as part of my job description. I would ask them to go to the job-site and get started. Evidently, they resented that! They wanted me right there alongside them doing the work with them! I didn't understand this because they were hired as service engineers and my job was to assist with the back end and come on-site if an extra hand was needed.

As the manager I was also responsible to meet with clients, strategize with the upper management handle all the paperwork I was required to process. They were fully trained and perfectly capable of being on their own, but they complained because they wanted more help. The VP thought I should be in the field on customer sites with the technicians when they were there, then handle the other work after hours. Again, rather than dealing directly with me on this issue, he brought it up in another team meeting blindsiding me stating my job was to be on site all day with them.

"But why?" I challenged, knowing I was growing red in the face again. "They are highly qualified adults. They know how to work. I'm their manager. I'm supposed to ... I have reports to do and business to grow my team is paid to do this work."

"But you need to help them, so you need to be there. Your job is to manage these guys not drive around making personal calls on your phone and trying to make half-hearted attempts to get more business."

So now there was an even bigger rift between me and my team because the guy at the top had created doubt and he had put me down in front of them again. I was feeling more and more like nobody respected me. What little self-confidence I had at work at the time was being eroded and any beliefs that these people were wrong were rapidly dwindling. They would just look at me and ignore me. It was a real struggle to think of myself as their boss. I felt like I was falling apart, and I started to feel like I deserved it. I later found that the VP was giving direction around me by instructing my team not to listen to me. I know that if I had been stronger at the time, I would have dealt with it all very differently, but I was in no shape then to redirect this or even fight back ... Then I lost the only real rock I had.

3

My dad was the best man at my wedding, my closest ally and biggest encourager. He was only 62 when he died. In the fall of 2000, I was driving to a meeting when I received that terrible phone call from one of my sisters.

My parents were heading out on a vacation trip to South Carolina and we had agreed to have lunch in Delaware the day they were leaving. Yet, I didn't hear from them until it was late in the day and the opportunity to see each other passed. My dad decided he wanted to take a more scenic route. At the end of that first day of their journey however, he got sick. My dad struggled through the night and the following morning he collapsed on the floor of the hotel room. My mom tried giving him CPR and worked to keep him alive; before the ambulance could get there however, he passed away in her arms. To say that this was another catalyst for the start of a lot of tumultuous years is an understatement.

When I was growing up, I felt close to my dad all the time. He was the disciplinarian if he needed to be, but he always seemed to be on my side. He was a great 'encourager' and somebody I always looked up to. He was very outgoing, with so many friends who loved him. He was just a happy guy who always wanted to have fun; the world was a big place and everything was exciting to him.

Getting over his death was hard. It took me a long time to accept that he was gone; that's when the real mourning set in. I felt like the wind was knocked out of me and I was not sure how to handle it. I would sit in the kitchen at night, unable to sleep just staring at the clock, wishing I could make the hands go backward so I could see him again. About 11 months later, I was just about getting back on my feet when the next family tragedy happened. This was on the morning of September 11th, 2001 when so many other families were destined to suffer horrendous loses as well.

We were expecting our second child, which, considering the state of the marriage, was very much unplanned, but the pregnancy had given us some respite and even some hope for the future. We went to the hospital that morning to check on the baby. At 19 weeks, my wife was concerned because she didn't feel any movement and she said something was wrong. Trying to reassure both of us, I said that there was nothing wrong with the baby, but we went to make sure.

Early that morning, we drove over to her parents' home so they could watch Louis while we were at the hospital. As we turned at the end of our street, we could see the Twin Towers, I made a big deal of it and pointed them out to him. It was such a beautiful bright and clear day we made a big fuss over seeing the sun sparkling on all the glass.

When we arrived at the hospital, we were eventually taken from the waiting area to a private room, where the nurse did an ultrasound scan. She was chatty and nice during the process, once she finished, she left the room.

"Oh, I just need to check something. I'll be back soon so just wait here," she said as she disappeared through the door.

"Probably our luck that the doctor will be doing an emergency C-section and we will be here all day," lamented my wife as we stood waiting for the nurse to return, wondering where she went. Not understanding how nervous she was about the status of our baby, I thought she was just complaining.

When the nurse came back in, she was acting very differently, actually quite sharp and said, "You will have to wait for your doctor, she is in the ER with an emergency C-section, so get dressed and wait outside again."

"Something's upset her," I said quietly, now fearing the worst about the baby.

"I don't know, but something is not right," agreed my wife, getting up off the bed.

Then the nurse came back in, but now she looked totally lost. Then she ran out of the room and a few moments later, came back. She said, "Oh, you need to see what is going on. We have been attacked. It's the Twin Towers."

My wife quickly finished dressing and we went back out to the waiting room where there was a TV and horrified like everyone else, we watched the events unfold until the nurse came to take us to see someone.

"We just want to leave. You know, with the circumstances, I want to get my son and take him home," said my wife.

"You can't leave," the nurse replied quietly, with tears in her eyes. "You need to wait for your doctor ... you see ... well, there is a problem with your baby, so you must wait to see the radiologist. Thing is... well, his brother works ... worked on one of the top floors of the first tower that was hit."

Too shocked to say anything, we followed the nurse into another room where a guy in his forties sat behind a desk. His face was dreadfully pale and his eyes were red from crying.

"I'm sorry to tell you this; I am having a hard ... My brother was on the 82nd floor of the first tower that went down. Well, I'm afraid you are going to have a hard day too. The thing is ... well, your baby has anencephaly, which means there is no brain. Your baby has a very slight ... very low percentage chance of being born alive and even lower chance of living. Really, I'd have to suggest ... well, termination ..."

As much as it wasn't an intended pregnancy, we had grown excited about our second child. We each looked at resolving this very differently. After much prayerful thought and discussion with family, we agreed with the doctor's recommendation.

Once we had accepted the baby would not live, we set the day to go to the hospital for the procedure. I remember the doctor being professional and serious and was grateful I didn't have his job in this situation.

I remained with my wife in the cold and sterile operating room and after the procedure was finished, we stayed the night in the hospital. Later, she admitted she was glad I was there and said she thought I might have just left her on her own. In the end, we were both physically and emotionally drained. The loss of our baby put a huge strain on the marriage. I took it hard and it took quite a while before I learned to live with the loss.

One morning soon after, my boss once more surprised me when he called me in to his office. "We need to make some changes to the team. You will be reporting to Daniel now," he calmly announced as he sat back in his chair, nursing his coffee.

"Danny! Why?" I said. I couldn't believe what I was hearing, so my remark must have come out a bit strong.

"Because I say so!" he retorted, almost spilling his drink. After he calmed down again he said, "I need someone to take some weight from me …"—he was famous for reading the sports page at his desk—"and this will be good experience for him."

"Exactly!" I said, getting more wound up. "I've got years more experience than him, and he's going to be managing me?"

"Yes he is, so you can help him by sharing your experience."

"So you want me to show my boss how to manage me?" I challenged, raising my voice again.

"Of course not!" he argued before he glossed over my question. "Daniel's worked very hard and he deserves a promotion, so that's that!" Daniel was also his after work drinking buddy.

I went back to my office feeling like the VP didn't know what to do with me, so his answer was to promote somebody who had even fewer skills. The guy had never had any leadership or management training let alone any experience and I was supposed to look up to him. It felt like all the VP wanted was to keep pushing me down because I was trying to grow. He didn't want me or the company to grow; perhaps he did want the latter, but not if I had a hand in it. At the time, I couldn't see that the best thing would have been to find a better environment to work in, but I didn't have the courage to even look, feeling like I wouldn't find anything better.

Danny was younger than me and very uptight. He was rigid in his ways and would talk in a cold nasally way while being condescending and hard on me. Because I was so emotionally sensitive then, everything would kind of make me jump a little. Even back in the days as a police officer, I never had to work with anyone like this guy. It seemed like he was trying to prove himself, he wanted everybody to think he was a tough military guy. He wouldn't have lasted a week in any Sheriff's Office.

A few weeks after he became my boss, I got called in to see him.

"It's time for your review, Lou."

"Really? That's not due for a few weeks."

"Well, I've accelerated it because I need to talk to you about your paperwork."

As it turned out, I had *literally* missed dotting an 'i' on a couple of pages! Then he stated that if I wanted to strike out a word that the line must be straighter and was instructed to use a ruler! He wrote all of this in my review to document these 'blatant' errors in my performance! Now as I look back, I think this was part of the set up for my demise. Then however, it felt more like he was right and I was wrong and it was difficult to maintain my perspective.

I forced myself to carry on and just keep my head down, but then, in early October 2003, it was announced that a major manufacturer in the region had purchased the company. Four weeks after that, on a Friday, Danny called when I was out at a site and for the first time, was nice to me. That was when he told me he wanted to meet me in the New Jersey office on Monday to discuss growing my region. That conversation we had on the Monday was so very different.

"With the takeover, we have some duplicate jobs, Lou and we need to let some people go."

"I thought you wanted to talk about growing the business?" I said already knowing that I was wasting my time. The new owners were a large public corporation that wanted to expand into our business so there would be no duplicate jobs; our company was just a new side to their portfolio.

"Well, we do, so then we had to decide who is going to leave."

"You never intended to talk to me about growth did you?"

"That's pointless now," he replied, the look on his face said it all. "Thing is, people have to go and… well because of the work you did for…" He named the company and my jaw dropped.

"You're firing me because I did an outside job?" I asked, my voice beginning to tremble. "How can you ignore all the good work I've done and my experience and knowledge that could be used in a business development role?"

"You're wasting your time, Lou, so let's not be stupid about this. You've got to understand our position so there's no need to look so upset."

What a callous bastard, I thought, turning bright red now with anger and embarrassment. I tried to argue down the seriousness of my 'crime'—which was again how it felt—but realized I was wasting my time. I had no non-compete or other agreement to follow, but I now could see that they considered it a 'conflict of interest'. Then, in my panic, I thoroughly belittled myself by talking about handing over the money I earned. As this was happening, I remembered that this was the Monday of the Thanksgiving holiday week.

"What's wrong, Lou? You look upset!" he questioned.

"You could have at least waited until after the holidays."

"Would it have made any difference?" he replied smugly. I really worked hard to maintain what little composure I had left to stop myself going for him over the desk. Instead, I decided I would not demean myself anymore, and I professionally handled the situation and offered a handshake with them.

"You'll give me time to clear my desk?" I asked. They simply nodded and walked out.

It was all so damned heartless when he knew I could lose my car and had mortgage payments to make. I tried to set up an appeal through the HR department, but even they wouldn't listen so at 12:20 pm on that Monday afternoon I went home to face the music there. All I could do as I drove through the rain was to keep telling myself how worthless I was; with so much stress inside, I felt like a pressure cooker about to explode.

4

Losing my job was the fundamental catalyst that opened my mind to the fact that there were so many other things going on, mostly in my head. These issues were messing with my life and causing me to feel uncomfortable, nervous and very unsure of myself. It was also the kick I needed to make the decision to start my own company, which later grew to become successful.

I knew there was something terribly wrong with my marriage, but that was just one part of it all. Although I didn't like the job, I had worked very hard and was sure I was worth much more. Yet, I had never expected to lose it. At the time I was fired, any sense of self-esteem I had been clinging to slipped away. I had no idea why. But I was going to find out, and little did I know it wasn't going to be easy.

On the day I was fired, I stopped along the way home to call a good friend and mentor. When I told him the news, he was empathetic, which did make me feel a bit better, until he asked me what I was going to do.

"Oh, I have no idea," I said. "My Amway income will help pay the mortgage, but it won't be enough to pay for everything."

"Well, if you will get focused, you can easily increase the income for that business."

My immediate response was excuse after excuse. "But you know there are just too many problems with that," I replied. "My wife hasn't been as interested in the business and I'm sure this will cause even more friction in our marriage. Besides, people on our Amway team are becoming more aware of our marital problems and are now focusing on them instead of their own businesses."

"Well then, I guess you'll just have to file for unemployment while you get your life together."

My response was, "I'll think about it" and ended the call, thanking him for his time. At first, I thought there was no way I would follow that last piece of advice, telling myself I didn't need it and only lazy people collected unemployment. I felt so worthless that I didn't even want to file for unemployment because I simply didn't feel I deserved it.

Then I called my wife and told her the news. She was understandably upset and very worried about how we were going to pay all our expenses. By the time I got home, she was more empathetic toward the situation we were in, which made me feel that our marriage could get better.

For some years, our relationship had been a rollercoaster ride. Some days were great and other days were terrible! Then again, that's how we existed; it was either black or white, there was never any middle ground. One day things seemed great, we were really in love and doing fine, the next I felt like a loser and I turned her off just by being in her presence.

I knew we needed counseling yet was afraid to go. My belief was that only people who had something wrong with them needed counseling; that couldn't be me. Why was I so worried about what other people would think of me if we had to get outside help to keep our marriage together? I tried to convince myself that we could handle this on our own, but eventually, it just became too difficult. If you ever think negatively about the idea of seeing a counselor, don't! Get professional help!

I reached out to my insurance network to find a counselor in my area. Initially, I thought I would see someone on my own. Part of me was afraid of what my wife would say about the idea of us getting counseling. My plan was to find a professional counselor, schedule an appointment and meet with them. If I thought they would be a good fit, I would then tell my wife all about it and ask her to join me. Not the best approach!

I met with the owner of the counseling center. Although it was extremely intimidating, I made my first appointment, knowing full well that we needed to take this step. The counselor he assigned me was an Italian woman from Jersey City. She was tough and blunt, typical "Jersey" but had a great sense of humor. In my first session, I explained the situation: I felt our marriage was in tenuous state and always feeling that I can never do anything right.

"Welcome to marriage!" she replied and even made me smile.

Then she turned serious again and asked what the key issues were: I told her that we were not communicating, and needed advice on how we can work together as a married couple.

"Why isn't your wife here?" she asked, looking me in the eye. I looked down and didn't answer.

"Does she know you're here?" she asked.

Shaking my head, I said, "Well, no. I was afraid to tell her, but besides, she wouldn't have come anyway."

Saying those words, sounded so weak. What type of man was I? I once was one of the toughest Training and SWAT officers at the Sheriff's Office?

The counselor closed the time, after hearing my observations of the marriage, she expressed that I may be in an abusive relationship. Her recommendation was that I tell my wife that I had a counseling session, then ask her to come with me to the next one. I waited a few days.

Driving home from a customer call in New York City one day, I was sitting in traffic and built up the courage to call my wife and tell her about the session. I was so nervous and shaking mostly, afraid of her reaction. After some routine discussion, I managed to let her know that I had gone to see a counselor. She was caught off guard, irritated with me and raised her voice.

"You have no right to do that! Why did you do that?"

Her question gave me the opening I needed to start talking, as the words came out, I started to feel better, although I really dreaded the face-to-face once I got home. For years, I always felt like there was something wrong with what I did or with me. It was never enough or perfect or what we needed. When I returned home, we continued the conversation. Unfortunately for me, there were more accusations against me.

"You set the bar and ask me to jump," I told her, "and then while I'm jumping, you move the bar and get mad at me because I missed it! If you keep moving the bar, how can I hit it?"

I told her I was deeply unhappy, it seemed to be the same for her as well. We needed help. I asked her to come to the next counseling appointment with me. My wife disagreed, saying that I was the one who needed the help and she put it off for a few months. But for me, this was the start of my journey to get healthy and overcome the lie that I was the only one with the problem.

Improvements in my emotional health became visible as I was setting boundaries in my life. People were noticing the change. Perhaps this was what prompted my wife's decision to join counseling with me. Perhaps there was hope.

Unfortunately, my wife found the counselor's style too abrasive and suggested we find someone who would be a better fit for us both. Because I wanted the marriage to work, I agreed, but I also continued with my Italian lady because I had built a trusting relationship with her.

"Lou, you are bending over so far backwards you're kissing your own ass!" she said to me one evening during a session.

That was how hard I was trying to make the marriage work—which wasn't improving, but slowly, painfully, I was. Or at least sometimes that's how I felt. Deep down, I felt like the marriage may need to end, but I didn't want to admit it. I had made a vow before God and agreed that we would be together "until death do us part."

Together my wife and I looked for another counselor, she found a Christian woman who we agreed to meet. My wife had her first session alone and told me afterwards. She then invited me to join the next session. I prayed that this was a positive sign; we were both going to attend together.

The office was in a converted home in our town. We found the office on the top floor and settled on a couch, with the counselor behind her desk. She turned to me and asked, "What's your daily routine?" I told her I woke early, prayed for 30 minutes, read, studied and exercised.

"What do you pray about?"

"I pray for my relationship with God, my wife, my son, my family and my business."

"And how much time is dedicated to praying for your wife?"

"About 5-10 minutes ..."

"You're not praying long enough for your wife," she reprimanded. "You must pray for her, on your knees, at least 30 minutes a day."

My emotions swirled around in my head from confusion to anger as the rest of the session turned into a lecture. There were no more questions from the counselor to understand my spiritual journey or our needs. Even more puzzling was that there were no more questions for my wife either. I wrote the check for the fee and neither of us went back.

5

I did increase my Amway business, but also managed to convince myself that I did deserve unemployment support. The company fought it, but in the end, I won. With the financial pressures eased a little, I decided that this was the opportunity I had been waiting for ... Since I had never signed a 'non-compete' agreement, I decided I would start my own company doing what I had been doing for my previous employer.

I called a friend I knew from the Amway business who managed a large diagnostics company lab. I told him I was starting my own service company and asked if I could come in to see him to talk about servicing their equipment. Knowing my values, my accomplishments in Amway and my work ethic, he agreed to have me stop by. He introduced me to coworkers as we walked through the lab. At one point, he showed me some equipment and asked if I could fix it; I told him I could. Even though I really didn't know what it was, I knew I would find someone to train me to repair that unit!

Within a year of starting the company, we were still facing large credit card debt, but the business was growing. I signed my first contract with that same large diagnostics company, which provided a bit of relief and hope that the business could thrive. To celebrate this milestone, I rewarded myself with a Tumi computer roller case. It was a little more than I planned to spend, but it served the dual purpose of carrying all my gear and laptop in one bag plus it was a reminder that I could win here!

My wife and I thought we would try a male counselor next, not thinking clearly, I suggested she might be more comfortable if she went in for the first session without me. When she returned, she stated, "He was fine. We need to go see him together." We scheduled for the following week.

As we settled in, the counselor started with a question, "Lou, tell me the reason behind making this totally unnecessary purchase of a computer bag. You're having money issues. Why spend this amount on a bag?"

I was shocked by the question. Maybe he planned to ask my wife about her spending habits, but either way, I felt judged because, he had gotten this from my wife, he knew nothing about the circumstances for me making the purchase.

"My company had just hit a major milestone by landing an annual contract. I needed a carrying case for all for my equipment and rewarded myself with the bag."

He did turn toward my wife, but instead of challenging her about her spending habits, he asked her why she refused to work even though our son was in school full-time. This was a fresh approach for me because the other counselors we saw placed the responsibility for the marriage troubles squarely on my shoulders. After this session, my wife decided this counselor wasn't a good fit!

I respected my wife's request to choose another counselor for us to visit jointly but I decided to see this man again, on my own. He seemed to understand something about me and I'm glad I listened to my gut feeling about him because the next session led to a very important discussion—he opened my eyes to what was happening.

He began with a list of questions, all of which prompted me to answer "yes." I wondered where this was going, then he got up from his desk and reached for a book from his shelf.

"Have you ever read this?" he asked me, handing me a paperback. I looked at the cover *Stop Walking on Egg Shells* by Paul Mason and Randi Kreger.

"Take a look at the introduction," he said.

When I started to read, it felt like a huge weight was being lifted. I wasn't going crazy. The authors described a condition called Borderline Personality Disorder or BPD. My counselor said, "I think this might be what you're dealing with."

My life changed that day. I was embarking on a significant life lesson with mountains to climb, but I had an advantage because of this new resource and would be better equipped to cope with the situation at home.

I am very grateful for this man and thank God that I didn't let his comments about my business and purchase of the Tumi bag put me off. I've found that I can learn from anyone whether we agree or disagree. This was a *huge* lesson for me: I frequently learn something from everyone I meet.

Following those revelations, I did research and studied whatever I could find about BPD. This disorder is very hard to detect and is one of the toughest personality problems to understand and live with. Most who exhibit these traits never feel they are wrong, admit to their problems or seek help.

During this period of my life, I was under an immense amount of stress. I was starting my company, going to counselors and working to help my marriage improve besides handling all the typical family issues. I would wake up at 6:00 a.m. to read, pray, and exercise and see Louis off to school. Then I would work all day, have dinner with my wife and son, spend some time with Louis or go out to continue to build the Amway business. When I got home again, we would put our son to bed and I would get to work establishing my company.

For months on end, I would work until 2:00 a.m. and sleep for just four hours a night. I conducted client research, prepared invoices, wrote contracts, established procedures, etc. I really needed help with the administrative side of the business and we still needed an extra income. My wife was only working a part time job, so if she worked with me when she wasn't working, I could bring in more business. I asked—even begged—several times that she join me, but she declined.

In between all this, I was doing laundry, cleaning our bathrooms and vacuuming. I was the assistant coach of my son's baseball team and the chairperson of his school's largest annual fundraiser. Where I found the energy and organization skills to handle all of this, God only knows. I was starting to feel like I was being spread too thin.

During one of her part-time jobs at an exclusive department store, my wife came home with a negative check. The first time I asked her what this meant. She stated that we needed some things, so she had put them on her account. She laughed it off. After a couple more of these checks, we couldn't afford for her to work at the department store any longer. I felt like we were paying the store to have her work. We discussed her getting a full-time job, but she said she wanted to be home to greet our son when he arrived home from school.

My company was growing to the point that if I didn't get some help, the company would crash. Fortunately, I was able to hire the daughter of a close friend of mine who was looking for a position like what the business needed. I knew that I would be able to trust her to do a good job and get me started. I had been desperate for my wife to help me, yet she refused. Once I hired an assistant, she accused me of wanting to have an affair with this girl! Despite the absurdity of her accusation and my loyalty to her, she continued to accuse me. Then she said she would have helped me if I had asked her! I was so grateful for the book the counselor had told me about or may have really gone crazy.

This was typical in our house. No matter what happened, there was always a reason that I was the one who screwed up. The answers usually changed so I could never do the right thing. One day, with all of this going on, I felt terribly stressed, as I sat at my desk, wondering what to do next, I kept hearing a sentence repeat in my head: "You are a piece of shit." It kept repeating over and over in my mind, and I just couldn't make it stop. I was so concerned I even asked my wife, "Why do I feel like a piece of shit?" She just looked at me as if the answer were obvious.

I just couldn't take the crazy unstable home life anymore and within a few days, I moved out of our house. This would be the first of *five times over the next four years* that I would leave and then return to our marital home. That first time, I went to live with my mom and I really felt like a loser. There I was, in my early 40's, physically fit, with a wonderful son, a nice house and the makings of a really successful company ... and here I was living with my mom.

In early March of 2005, things finally came to a head. One night before bed while staying at my mother's house, I was on my knees, face towards the floor as I prayed, suddenly I had a vision of some type of reaper standing over me holding a large, ancient looking sickle. This repeated over the next few nights. I just couldn't shake off the image and it was really starting to freak me out. I was petrified and would have distressing dreams once I did manage to get to sleep.

I had no idea what to do or how to stop the visions and the dreams! I knew I needed to talk to someone, so I called a friend, a man named Charles who was a Messianic Christian with a background in counseling. I thought he might know about the wild things, like those I was experiencing. I first met Charles in 2003 when we were introduced by a mutual friend who was a church pastor with whom I had gotten to know through my Amway business. Charles was not a priest or someone working in the church, but he had made a lifelong study of the Scriptures. He was the president of an oil and gas company based in Oklahoma, yet I was sure he was the right person to contact. It turned out that I was right.

Once I got him on the phone and explained the situation, he began asking me some questions, but his questions were different. As I answered, I started tingling with intense fear, I told him that at one point, I thought my mom was going to kick down the bedroom door and kill me! This, coming from SWAT cop who was usually the first one going through the door to take down someone else! He told me several things, but there was one that really hit me hardest.

"You know, Lou, there is always a reason for the stuff we get in our heads."

"I guess so, but I have no idea where all of this is coming from.

"Well … I need to talk to you face to face and not on the phone; I'm starting to think I know where this is coming from."

"Really?" It was neither an argument nor an acceptance but simply an acknowledgment of what he said. It also felt like a straw I could clutch at.

"Yeah, Lou. I think … well, I'm quite sure actually … I think you were abused when you were a child."

This came as such a shock and I wanted to scream in denial— my family life had been all about loving and caring.

I first responded with; "I wasn't abused. I was a cop! How could I have been abused?"

"Well, you weren't a cop when you were a child …"

"Oh…yeah" I said.

Now, I humbly listened, and he said that, from my answers to his questions, it seemed like I was exhibiting different personalities, which related to fragmented memories. He questioned me further and asked about my past and I realized that I couldn't recall things from a certain period in my life. This, he said, was a way of blocking out hurtful memories. This too was another sign of abuse.

Because of the intense fear I was feeling, he told me to leave my mom's that night, to find a hotel where I might get some sleep, then fly out to meet him in Oklahoma the next morning.

"Tomorrow morning?" I asked doubting all of what I heard... I wanted to argue this extreme approach because the 'okay' side of me said I was fine, a SWAT cop who would outperform all my teammates when it came to my duties and physical activities. How could I have been abused? I was in denial and very afraid of what I would face next, but in the end I agreed.

PART 2

CHILDHOOD

*"Be strong and **courageous**. Do not be afraid or terrified because of them, for the LORD your God goes with you; he will never leave you nor forsake you." Deuteronomy 31:6*

6

"Louie, Louie, I gotta go out and run some errands," shouted Mom from the hallway.

"Is Dad coming back now?" asked Louis from his bedroom.

"No, he's busy at the store. Your uncle's not working today, so I called him and he's coming over."

Louis didn't respond. Fear overcame him.

"Louis? Did you hear me?"

"Yes Mom," he replied quietly. "Can I come with you? Please?"

"No, you need to stay inside. You're not ready to go out yet."

Louis had tonsillitis and needed to be quiet and rest. His sisters were over at his grandmother's house, so he wouldn't get overexcited. He was almost ready to go back to pre-school but needed a few more days.

As he pushed cars around the floor, Louis wished his mom had taken him with her. He didn't like his uncle and especially didn't like being alone with him.

Louis lived with his family, his mom, dad and younger sisters, in a small house on a very short dead-end street in New Jersey. There were three houses on each side of the street; theirs was in the middle on the right-hand side. It was quiet neighborhood in a stable middle-sized town. Louis' paternal grandfather, the son of an Italian immigrant and one of five children, had moved to this town years before.

His grandfather had started a retail business in 1942 as a printer, which had grown to become very successful. He was well known and liked by many people and sat on the board of directors at the local bank. He was involved in several other organizations like the Lions Club and helped many of his friends and family members become successful and wealthy. As a child of the depression, he was conservative in his lifestyle and lived with Louis' grandmother in a very modest apartment behind their store. He owned that building and several others, as well as two or three homes, which provided rental income. His home was humble, comfortable and well kept.

He paid cash for his cars and kept them for six or more years. When he had multiple coupons for items at the grocery store, he would use all of them. He would make several trips throughout the day, using different checkout lines to be able to cash in on all the savings. He tried to go unrecognized, but everyone knew him and knew what he was doing, yet, they always welcomed him. He was one of those people that just seemed popular with everyone. He was amicable and encouraging with those he met.

Both of Louis' grandparents were relatively short, around 5'8". His grandfather was a good-looking man of average build with dark, thick hair and his grandmother was a little bit heavier with thinning hair. She was a homebody who worked in their store stocking shelves, filling the numerous phone orders, taking inventory and helping retail customers when necessary. She was one of 13 children and liked being around her family, always talking about them and frequently visiting with them. They had two children and Louis' father broke the family mold to become 5'10". His older brother was a little shorter; he was the one who was to play such a major part in young Louis' life and was the one who would have the greatest impact on the boy's future.

After high school, Louis' father went straight into the Army and worked his way up to Sergeant. He met Louis' mother, his wife, on a blind date. He was a devout Catholic and made sure the family attended church every Sunday as well as ensuring the children attended the local Catholic school. Louis' father loved and respected his parents. He helped whenever they asked, and would cover the store for them, if needed, while his brother was off enjoying himself, which would be a common event.

The house on the dead-end street had a small, but pleasant back yard, with a blackberry bush and a large apple tree. It was here that Louis and his sisters had fun with the family's large and much-loved pet dog, an over-protective German Shepherd named Chancellor. He was huge even by adult size standards and would only allow a few people, besides Louis' mom and dad, around his sisters and him—the boy's grandmother his uncle and another one or two family members.

For all other family members or friends who came to visit, including Louis' grandparents on his mother's side, Chancellor would have to be locked up on the back porch. Louis and his sisters, but especially Louis, loved playing with the Shepherd. He was a big tough dog, but he allowed the kids to pull on him, hug him, and even sit on and ride him. Just lying on the floor next to him was fun since his large, furry stomach made a soft and comfortable pillow.

Louis' mom loved everyone dearly and would make sure she always took great care of their home, her husband and children. She was very creative, always looking for ways to improve the look of her home. Occasionally, she would take ceramics classes and learn other crafts, so she could make new things to brighten and decorate the place.

When it came to family and church, his mom held the same beliefs and values as her husband. Except for their weekly bowling nights away from the kids, the family typically had dinner together and attended Mass every weekend. She raised her young family, while still helping her own mom who was sick and living nearby. Louis' maternal grandmother finally succumbed to brain cancer in 1968, which was the same year the family moved away from what had truly become a little house of horrors.

Louis' uncle, on his dad's side, was a muscular man who rolled up his shirt sleeves to show his biceps, even when he was wearing a button-down shirt. He was good looking, with dark wavy hair. He acted like he owned the world but had nothing to back it up. Always showy and flashy, he had cheated his way through Villanova University, openly bragging about breaking into an office to steal final test papers so he and his friends could pass their exams. Even though he later married, he was the playboy type who always liked being around young women, treating them like objects to use for his pleasure.

Despite these shortcomings, possibly because he was the first born, Louis' grandmother made it clear that his uncle was her favorite. He was the opposite of Louis' father. When Louis was in his early teens, he began to witness and understand the favoritism himself. By then, the evil, vicious things he had experienced in his childhood years were now buried deep in his subconscious mind.

In Louis' earliest years, usually his grandmother or uncle would look after the children whenever their parents were out. His grandmother didn't drive so his uncle, or another family member would drive her over. To Louis, it seemed like his uncle was always there.

When Louis' uncle turned up on that dreadful afternoon when he had been sick, Louis could tell by the look in the man's eyes that something bad was about to happen again! Immediately, the boy wanted to be somewhere else and wished, for the hundredth time, that his uncle wasn't one of the people that the dog let near him. His uncle's face had a frightening sheen to it and an expectant look in his eyes. Louis wondered what horrors might unfold that day; he was already afraid he might wet himself; sometimes the anticipation of the abuse was worse than whatever viciousness might be planned.

While looking out the window, Louis saw that there was

someone else with his uncle, a woman had gotten out of the car who he had never seen before. She had bright blonde hair like he had seen in pictures of Marilyn Monroe and the same large chest that seemed to have a life of its own. *Who was this woman and what was she doing here?* Louis was curious, but there was no warmth in the woman's smile when she saw him peering around the drapes. For some reason, she scared him more than his uncle. Then he heard the dog start to grumble under his breath.

His uncle had a key and let himself into the house to lock the dog up before he let the woman in.

"Where's that little shit?" he shouted. Louis just sat frozen and terrified on the floor behind the drapes.

"Come on little shit. I brought someone to meet you."

Louis heard the woman giggle and he thought she sounded like one of his little sisters. The door opened and they walked in, his uncle strutting like a peacock and the woman teetering on her high heels. His uncle walked over, lifted the drapes, and kicked Louis on the leg to make him get up.

"I was about to have some fun with Charlene when your mom spoiled it, so I brought her to have some fun here, instead. You can watch and learn!"

Afraid of what was about to happen he said, "I want to go and play in the yard."

"I said you'll stay here!" shouted his uncle and Louis flinched. "Now go sit in that chair," he added, pointing at an armchair.

Louis did as he was told and at just four years old, he was forced to watch as his uncle and the woman have sex. But it wasn't 'making love' kind of sex; it was ugly and violent as his uncle roughly grabbed the woman's hair and pushed himself into her mouth. Then she screamed and shouted as his uncle repeatedly rammed himself into her from behind as she leaned over the sofa.

"Maybe I'll do this to you next you little shit!" he panted, his eyes made him look like he was possessed. Louis sat there petrified wondering if his uncle would do just that!

7

Louis had always felt nervous around his uncle, even when the entire family was together, but no one else picked up on this and Louis never told anyone. Unfortunately for Louis, his uncle was not the only one who abused him! The first time it happened, his uncle was there, but the perpetrator was his paternal grandmother. Perhaps that was why his uncle—*always* her favorite son—could get away with the horrible things he did. As a young boy, Louis couldn't figure out how people could be so cruel, especially his grandmother and uncle. Family is supposed to love and support each other or so he thought!

Sometimes Louis' uncle and grandmother would team up to torment him. One time his uncle had sex with Charlene, the large breasted woman, while his grandmother was present … she sat in a chair, looking back and forth, watching Louis then watching them. But it was his grandmother who started things in the basement of the house, with his uncle watching *her*. Louis was very young, but old enough to have horrific images seared into his brain.

Louis was walking around playing while his grandmother was taking care of him; his uncle was also in the house. The uncle came into the room and nodded his head.

"Come here, Louie," she said. The boy walked over, totally trusting.

She picked him up, looked at Louis' uncle and then nodded. His uncle walked over to the door to the unfinished basement that his parents rarely used, and they took him down the creaky stairs. Louis didn't like the basement because it was dark and dirty, but he felt safe in his grandmother's arms and did not cry. Then he heard a chicken start to squawk.

The house used to belong to a man who did a lot of engineering work and made things with metal. For some reason, there were chains hanging from the ceiling, and his uncle hung the chicken up by its legs. As it wriggled and squirmed, Louis was held aloft in his grandmother's arms. He started crying as he was hoisted into some wires that joined the chains. He was left suspended next to the distraught chicken.

Now, his so-called "good Catholic" grandmother lifted her arms and began a ritualistic chant as his uncle slashed the neck of the chicken and it bled out on a plastic sheet they had put on the floor; splashes of blood speckled across Louis and he screamed and screamed, wholly terrified. This 'ceremony' was repeated several times in Louis' earliest years and the minute he was taken over to the stairs, he would begin to scream. Hoping for someone to help him.

One time, when he was a little older, Louis was hanging, in a suspended cradle sobbing when he saw his sister hiding, under the unfinished wooden staircase looking petrified. The worst time was the first. When there was a man with a dark suit and overcoat present in the room. The man wore a large hat, so Louis could not see his face, but he was very afraid of him. The man never moved or said anything, and Louis neither knew who or what he was or why he was there … this gave him terrible nightmares. The worst things that were done though were by his uncle when the two were alone.

A couple of weeks after his uncle had sex in front of Louis with the big busted woman, he was there one evening when Louis' parents had gone out bowling. The children were in bed, his sisters asleep, but Louis had a bad cough and needed some water. He tried to sneak into the kitchen to get a glass, but his uncle was already in there, drinking beer and reading a newspaper.

"What do you want shit?"

"Only a drink. I need some water."

"Well, hurry up and get out!"

Louis got a glass from the drainer by the sink; he was not big enough to get one from the cupboard. He turned the glass over to hold it under the faucet when, because it was still wet from washing, it slipped from his fingers and crashed to the floor. Louis burst into tears, both from the shock of the sudden explosion of glass and because he knew his uncle would fly into a rage.

"You piece of shit!" screamed his uncle. "You are totally useless and I hate you! Get out of here, I hope you choke to death!"

"I didn't mean it. I'm sorry. I only wanted a drink."

"Don't you argue with me shit!" screamed his uncle, this time so loud he woke up Louis' sister, which threw him into an even bigger rage.

"Now look what you've made me do! Now I've got to quiet your brat of a sister down too. God, I hate you and wish you would leave me alone!"

With that, he grabbed Louis roughly by the ear and dragged him out to the hallway. Louis knew immediately where he was being taken and wanted to struggle, but the pain in his ear was too much. His uncle yanked open the basement door and without turning the light on, threw Louis down the stairs.

"And I hope you die!" he screamed as the small boy tumbled helplessly down into the darkness. Then the door was slammed shut.

8

By the time Louis' parents came home, he was back in bed and his uncle had threatened to kill Louis' sister if he said anything to his parents. He lay there, shaking and still sobbing, as he heard his parents speaking to his uncle in the hallway.

"Louis had an accident tonight," said his uncle.

"What do you mean?" asked his mom anxiously.

"Did he ever sleep-walk before?"

"Not that I know of," replied his dad.

"Well, he went sleep walking tonight and for some reason, he opened the basement door and fell down the stairs."

"He what?" replied his mother. "Is he alright?"

"Oh, he's in bed again now, nothing broken and just a few bruises. Banged his ear and that's a bit red, but he's okay."

"Well, I'm going to check on him. How long have I been telling you to put a lock on that door?" she continued.

"Well I'm going to do it tomorrow," he heard his dad say as his mom walked into his bedroom.

When he was small, Louis could never understand why his uncle hated him so much, but he was always told he was useless and called a "piece of shit". This happened so much that Louis started to believe that it was true. There was a very strong dynamic in Louis' broader family that people respected their elders and children most certainly listened to adults and did exactly what they were told. In his heart, Louis knew that he was not a bad child; his parents only scolded him if he really did something wrong.

Sometimes when he was at school, his teacher, an older nun,

would lose her temper and shout at the class in general, but Louis usually felt it was only him that was a target of her anger. When he got home, he sometimes told his parents that the teacher had shouted that day, and without asking for details, his father would immediately ask:

"Well, what did you do? What did you do to deserve that?"

They were just thinking he was a normal boy, but this reaction and behavior from his parents inadvertently endorsed what he felt in class, pushing him further into that downward spiral that left him feeling that everyone only wanted to accuse him of things, whether he had done them or not. It perpetuated a cycle of guilt that was further endorsed by his strict Catholic upbringing; everyone appeared to feel guilty about everything that happened.

Some Friday nights and Saturday mornings — his parents went bowling. When he was a little older, he would join them on the weekend, but those earliest evenings meant being left with his grandmother or, mostly, his uncle.

As much as his uncle seemed to hate Louis, he seemed to really enjoy abusing him and would encourage Louis' parents to go out even more with a, "Hey, I'll watch the kids." If they weren't around, he could have his fun. Unfortunately for Louis, the sexual abuse was eventually turned towards him.

One night, he was asleep when his uncle came in and woke him up. He was carrying a magazine with lots of pictures of women with no clothes on and as he sat on the bed and stared at the images, he forced his erect penis into the Louis' mouth. After that, it would happen more often. Louis was terrified, sickened, and traumatized, but if that was what an adult told him to do, then that's what he did. Louis often wondered if his uncle ever did anything with his sisters.

Louis' mom didn't get along that well with his paternal grandmother. That was mostly due to how brazen she was about his uncle being the favorite and how demanding she was about being 'respected' as the matriarch of the family. His dad would be routinely criticized, but *never* his uncle. Unfortunately, the constant criticism never triggered any suspicion in his parents that the older woman was abusing Louis in her disturbing rituals, or that she might be condoning the abuse handed out by his uncle. Louis realized his parents never knew about the abuse that he had suffered, because they were always very protective of all their children. But, of course, he accepted that, as horrible as it was, his uncle was *right* to do such things as he was the adult and Louis was taught to respect his elders.

Louis was born in 1963 and three sisters followed, the last being born in 1967. A year later, his parents knew they needed a much bigger place, so they purchased a home with three bedrooms, a full and finished basement and a two-car garage; they later expanded it to five bedrooms. By this time, Louis was almost six and with the move to the different house, the abuse diminished. Perhaps this was because his uncle was more concerned about the child talking about what happened, or maybe even the old house had been evil in some way and needed exorcising. Whatever the reason, Louis began to push the memories of those times deeper and deeper into his subconscious, to be forgotten until they started to resurface in 2004.

Just before they left the old house, his uncle wanted to remind Louis of what he thought of him. There was one last session of abuse. Fortunately for Louis, it only consisted of his uncle throwing dog feces on him and locking him in the closet as he called him a "piece of shit." This phrase was to keep repeating in his head when, years later, his life literally fell apart.

PART 3

UPHILL CLIMB

"Forgiveness is not an occasional act, it is a constant attitude."

- Martin Luther King Jr.

9

"You okay bud?" asked the taxi driver as I settled into the back of his cab. I must have appeared to the cab driver like I felt. It was a little after 6:00 a.m.

I was sitting in the back of the cab recalling the conversation that I had with Charles the previous evening about my mom kicking in my door and trying to kill me.

"Yeah, I'm okay. Just had a bad night with not much sleep."

"Oh right!" he replied as he grinned in the mirror. "Big night eh? Lots of booze and ladies!"

"Yeah, something like that. Airport, please. Domestic."

"You got it bud," he said as he pulled out of the hotel parking lot.

I was not going to correct him as to why I looked and felt so frazzled. That I had been trying to get my head around what Charles had suggested. My mom and dad were wonderful, so how could I have been abused? None of it made any sense and the more I tried to rationalize it, the more confused I became. I just felt so tired, yet I could not sleep.

The flight to Oklahoma lasted four hours, but it seemed like a lifetime. It was as if my life had been filmed and I was watching it back in slow motion. I needed to talk to Charles and begin to get my head around his suggestions. I couldn't do it on my own. I barely touched the breakfast I was served, simply sipping a couple of cups of coffee; I knew I should eat but couldn't face any food.

Charles lived in Colorado but was working at his corporate headquarters in Oklahoma for the week. After he picked me up from the airport, he took me to the hotel to unpack and get freshened up, then we went to his office. He told me later that he could see I was in bad shape, so he wanted to impart some normalcy. He took me to his office and introduced me to some people. I managed to chat and forget about things for a little while as I waited for him. He simply described me as a colleague and friend who was visiting. His people warmly greeted me and explained how the oil and gas business worked and what the company was doing. Charles knew exactly what he was doing because this helped me focus on something besides my inner turmoil and myself.

Around 4:30, he came by saying he was ready to go. I said goodbye to the folks I had been sitting with, thanked them for their time and we went outside to his car.

"You hungry?" he asked as he drove out onto the street.

"Not really. Where are we going? Get something to eat?"

"We'll head back to the hotel, since you're not hungry now, we can get some room service later." Charles was staying at the same hotel for the week since he was in Oklahoma on business.

"So, we're … we're going to talk in my room?"

He glanced at me, probably sensing something in my voice. One side of me was really intrigued to explore what he suggested, but the other side of me was extremely afraid of what was going to come out.

"Yeah, we will, but don't worry. We'll start with some prayer and then take it from there. See how it goes. See what we can find in the Bible to help."

"Okay," I replied as I stared out of the window, watching the rush hour traffic go by.

Up in the hotel room, we got settled, him in the chair and me sitting on the edge of the bed. We prayed for a while, asking God for His guidance and help for me as we sought to address what was burdening me. Then Charles marked a few passages in the Bible he wanted to refer to as we went through things.

"You know Lou, if you want God's help to get you through all this, then you've got to have the right relationship with Him. Okay?"

"Go on."

"It's got to be an honest relationship, where He sees He can trust you. He already knows everything that has happened in your life. He needs to know that you want to cleanse yourself of any sins from your past, to seek His forgiveness and start things anew. Does that make sense?"

It did. Years earlier I had accepted Jesus as my Savior, but this was a little frightening and confusing. What sins was he talking about? Would I be forgiven from all of them?

"I guess so, but where do I start?"

"How about letting go of some of your past relationships?"

"How do you mean?"

"Well, have you ever had intimate relations with other women before your marriage?"

I simply nodded my head in understanding and that was my start of remembering and admitting all the sins that I could list. Those first steps were for me to talk about my "intimate relations" with women before I was married. As a result, there were still some type of ties or connections ... maybe a soul connection. I was simply admitting that I knew it was wrong and that it had not been the best decision for me.

Over the coming days, other things followed. They might have been sins or simple mistakes like holding onto things that happened to me or things I did to others, but I had to get everything out into the open. In the evenings, I was so afraid. I felt like the Grim Reaper was waiting for me at the end of the hotel hallway. That feeling started to haunt me back in New Jersey and I felt like he would be waiting for me when I arrived in Oklahoma. Fortunately, there were two queen-sized beds in my room. One night the fear was so bad I called Charles and asked him to bunk in the room with me. He graciously agreed and brought some music to help me sleep.

The way we approached each session was that I had to confess to all the events, actions of past relationships and other sins that I tried to hide from God and myself. I had buried all the old negative emotions and carried them with me throughout my life. Now during these sessions, I needed to ask for forgiveness. I needed to 'admit' to everything and to be honest with God *and* myself.

"This is so very important, you know," encouraged Charles as I struggled with the confusion in my head. "The reason why you're doing this is getting you to be honest and trust yourself. I'm certain now some things are going to come out, that you are going to talk about, that you're not going to believe. You're going to expose memories that have been buried that you won't want to remember, but you've got to be able to consider that what you're telling yourself is true. You are not going to bring up and say things that aren't true or raise problems that never really happened. It's all about honesty and if you trust and believe God, then He will *faithfully* help you."

At the beginning of these exercises, I still felt so worn out and tired that I didn't feel any change in myself, but the more I asked God to cut off the soul ties from those women and to forgive the other things I had done, the more the relief began to come. I even felt better physically! Once I truly opened the doors, it was like the snowball had gone from laboring down a shallow hill to rolling down a large mountain gaining size and momentum. But this didn't come without a lot of effort and not just from me; for that, I will always be eternally grateful to Charles, my friend and mentor.

After that first series of sessions, Charles was scheduled to be in Oklahoma a month later. We had just scratched the surface of the memories, so I scheduled a return trip. We were spending between four to six hours a day in these sessions. At times, it was exhausting yet I was starting to feel somewhat better. One benefit was that I was finally able to sleep. When I was awake, I would either follow Charles around during his workday or on occasion I would just hang out, walk around outside or in the park to get some fresh air and relax while I waited for Charles to finish his workday.

One day, near the middle of my second visit to Oklahoma, it was raining, I'd been walking aimlessly through a mall as I tried to get my head clear on all that I had learned. When I later met up with Charles, I sought to clarify my thinking at the end of our session.

"So, what you're saying is that if someone can deal with the problems that they've had in the past and release the pain, then they will be able to have a more honest future relationship, not only with God but with themselves and others. They need to be honest with themselves about what happened in their past and when they do, they can be more honest with themselves about their life in the future?" I asked.

"Yeah, that's a great way to say it, Charles responded. People in your situation need to have integrity about everything in their lives, to be totally honest and learn to trust themselves."

Once we were both comfortable that I now had that clean slate, it was time to move forward and the next thing we did was look at my family line, my lineage.

"You know Charles," I said as I came back from the bathroom and sat on the bed again. "Before I spoke to you that night from my mom's when you suggested the abuse, I had been talking to a cousin on the phone. Somehow, she heard that I was going through a rough patch; we've always been close, so she called me to see how I was doing. She had a few problems of her own and knew of a few other family members with similar problems. She felt that none of these problems were surprising!

"So why was that?" he asked.

"You know, I had never known this, but my cousin started telling me about all the incest in my paternal grandmother's side of the family. My cousins' father, (another uncle) was having sexual relations with his brother's (another uncles) wife, I guess he and his brother were swapping wives. Then my cousin told me about my dad's brother (the man who abused me) and one of our cousins. She explained that when they were in their 40's and even into their 50's, they would pick-up college girls and take them to Atlantic City to gamble, have sex and do drugs."

As well as looking shocked at all this, Charles got a little excited and grabbed his Bible from the top of the desk beside him, without saying a word, he began thumbing through the Old Testament. He found and read the passage he was looking for and then looked up.

"What I'm getting a sense of now is that your family has what we call a generational curse on it. I already strongly believed that we were going to uncover sexual as well as other abuse in your childhood and there is also incest. Could the abuse, which we've just started to uncover, have come from your grandmother's side of the family?"

At that time, I had no reason to know if I was right, but I firmly nodded my head and began to feel terrible again. I felt guilty. I felt bad, I felt dirty, and I felt shameful. I felt all those things, but I had no idea why. If I accepted Charles' suggestion, I came from a family with a generational curse!

10

Because of how the cruelty of any abuse is attached to one physically, spiritually, and emotionally—through the body, mind and the soul, Charles and I began to work on healing my body and soul by using a system called "Theophostic Ministries". (Now called Transformation Prayer Ministry). Charles had been through training in the system and sent me some videos to watch so I would have a better understanding of the process. He used this process and other things to help me release those old destructive memories.

"Remember what we talked about Lou, you need to ask God to cut those soul ties. So, here's what I want you to do. We are going to go back in time, not through hypnosis or anything like that, but to open your memory. We're going to use God's help through Theophostics to draw out each incident and once we have it then I'm going to ask you to picture scenes or memories from your past. Knowing that Christ is and was always with you, I want you to describe your memory as you remember it happening. As you relive it in your mind, I want you to describe what you are seeing. I want you to tell me who is with you and where they are in the scene."

Charles allowed me to explain what I was seeing and feeling during these sessions. He was careful not to use suggestive language or put images into my subconscious, but he would guide me to come to realization and acceptance. He would encourage me and kept saying:

"Just tell me what you see. Tell me what you're experiencing."

So, for the first time since all the memories I buried from my early childhood, I began to relive each event right there in my mind. Once I started, it was like a snowball effect, so many events were coming out—too many for one session—so I just started with what came up first since that was, perhaps, the most important.

It was truly horrific, like recalling one's worst nightmares, but I would call each memory up and do my best to bring it to life. I told Charles about getting pushed down the stairs; about my grandmother holding me up and putting me up on the chains in the ceiling; about the man in the dark suit—all of that came out. I sobbed uncontrollably as I explained about my uncle having violent sex with a woman in my presence and making me watch. I talked about him forcing himself on me and how, so many times, he called me a "piece of shit." All of that was discovered as it was revealed to me for the very first time over those initial days with Charles in that Oklahoma hotel room.

As the memories that I had buried for so long reappeared, I was in a terrible state. I was sweating and I was scared. I was nervous. I was crying. I was hurt and I was mad. I was angry with God, wondering how He could have let things like that happen to a young child.

"Where were you when I was being abused, Lord?" I felt dirty and guilty like all of it was *my* fault! Then came the shame.

Charles told me later how hard it was for him to listen to my experiences and feel as if he was being so cruel by making me relive the horrific abuse. Charles stayed strong and kept me going! He would keep telling me that "if we get it all out in the open, we can deal with it"—without his encouragement, I could never move forward from the low point at which I found myself. I had to hit the bottom before I could start to climb back up.

As I was going through the process, Charles would continually ask about what and who I saw. I finally saw Him! Jesus was there with me, I wasn't alone! He was there! Now knowing that I was not alone, I was able to work through the memory and once again experience my uncle and the woman having sex in front of me.

"So where is He now?" Charles urged me yet again, defying me to not see Him.

"I don't see Him; I don't see Him!" I cried, my eyes firmly shut as my whole body shook.

"Okay, I want you to stay calm. I want you to know you're alright," Charles reassured me. "It's okay; this happened a long time ago and is over now. It's not going to happen anymore. This is not happening now; it is only a memory, but I want you to see it again, so you can know *Jesus* was *always* with you. Now, can you see Him in that scene?"

I could see my uncle and the woman on the sofa, and then it happened, in the doorway to the dining room, I could see a figure, an image of Christ, a very bright and typical Christian image, but it was not like a two-dimensional photograph. He was real, the fourth person in that room, the warmth and love that radiated from Him was unbelievable. I felt like He was protecting me, even during all that abuse.

That was an amazing moment and once I described what I was seeing to Charles, the image of the whole scene faded, and I opened my eyes.

"So, He was there with you through all of the abuse?" asked Charles, and I nodded my head. "What we are saying is that Jesus chose not to intervene to stop what was happening, but He was there with you, to comfort you and to see you through it."

"So, Christ also helped me forget?" I asked as I wiped my eyes, and Charles shrugged his shoulders briefly.

"Who can say Lou, but when we're young and these terrible things happen, as a protective mechanism our minds tend to bury them, push them down. Then, as we get older, our body and mind changes and you just can no longer suppress the memories. Something happens—like you getting fired—which is like reaching the end of a fuse that has been fizzing for a long time. Because you were under so much stress and so tired, your defenses broke down, and you started getting these thoughts about feeling like a piece of shit."

All that, quite simply, made total sense to me. The memories being buried, but then being resurrected when I was older and could deal with them, was part of a natural 'process'. I had to feel the hurt before I could heal and needed to accept what happened before I could go through the entire process of recovery and feeling 'normal' again.

That was my belief then and what my experiences subsequent to that time have confirmed. These views were also very much supported by Charles. He knew how bad things would become, so by getting me involved in his daytime routines, he was seeking to distract me, filling me with a sense of normalcy at the same time. In the evenings, we would come back to my problems, but during the day he wanted to keep me grounded in the here and now.

By the time Charles and I agreed I was ready to go back home; I was still raw and feeling kind of lost, having just stirred up over 40 years of horrendous memories. I was devastated about having been abused, which brought about embarrassment and shame that I sought to hide, knowing full well that also had to keep things together for my son when I got back to New Jersey.

On the flight back, I wasn't feeling so good, I started feeling terribly claustrophobic, something I never experienced before. I thought I was going to lose it or flip out. I struggled to my feet and went to use the restroom. I talked calmly to myself as I looked in the mirror, telling myself I was going to be okay, I was taking steps in the right direction. After feeling in control, I went back to my seat.

Trying to keep my mind in the present, I just stared out the window and calmly tried to reassure myself. I was afraid to go back home and unsure of what life would be like now, because I felt very different. I felt like I had when coming home from a SWAT training where we were immersed in simulated danger for extended periods of time. The situations mimicked reality from tactical planning to shooting and forming new mindsets to deal with hostile situations. I was on high alert for days after a training and had to process through that emotion. I felt like that now and managed to calm myself, but remained nervous because everything was boiling up inside me. I knew I was changed after the sessions with Charles and that I would need time to work through what I had learned.

After I landed back in New Jersey, I went back to my mom's and stayed there for a little while, but then I got an apartment on my own with a six months' lease. I set up a bedroom for my son, so he could stay a few nights each week because he couldn't be with me all the time. The alternative would have been going back to live with my wife, but I was in no state for that and neither was our marriage.

When I was on my own, I was very lonely because I felt beaten and broken from the emotion of all the memories. I still had so much fear inside of me as if I were four or five years old again. Sometimes I would curl up on my mattress on the floor and stare at the wall. I would pray and listen to personal development CD's. Some from Amway some from Napoleon Hill and some from Brian Tracy whose calming voice and youthful insights helped me focus on growing and getting through this mess.

The daytime was better because I was diligently working on building my new company, which offered calibration services to diagnostic and pharmaceutical companies. I was also very involved with my son's school and spent a lot of time with him, which was very healing even though I was still mentally and emotionally drained.

Working on my business, which alone was probably 12 hours a day, meant going back to the marital home at times because that's where my office was located, but either my wife was out, or if she was home, we spoke as little as possible, mostly about our son. I did try to tell her about my experiences in Oklahoma, but she didn't want to know.

Charles and I stayed in touch, on a regular basis, once I returned home from my first trip. These conversations helped me stay grounded. On the second and last trip to Oklahoma, Charles met me at the airport and as soon as I got in the car, he wanted to know in more detail about how I had been. After I told him about how things were going and did my best to answer his questions, he told me what he wanted to focus on next.

"I've been doing a lot of reading, studying and meditating and I want us to tackle this generational curse. We need to do that as part of your own healing process, but more so we need to do it for your son," Charles said.

"So how do we do that? Are you sure it'll work?" I asked, getting scared again. This time it was for my son more than for myself.

"I'll give you the details later, but the research I've done suggests it should work. We need to ask God for His help and trust in Him. I also need you to call your wife and tell her that as we go through this process, something might happen to your son, he may get sick in some way, but it's okay. Don't tell your son anything, just tell your wife in case something happens and reassure her that he is going to be fine."

Even though my wife didn't like Charles for many reasons, I did as Charles asked and let her know that Louis may experience possible effects while Charles and I go through the process of releasing generational curses. I simply told her she had to be aware that it may or may not affect our son and that was that. The following day, we reconvened in my hotel room and went into the process that Charles had thoroughly researched.

"We'll read a particular verse from within the text of *Deuteronomy 28:15-68,*" explained Charles, "and then you will say that you rebuke this curse. You'll state your parents' full names and then say you add all their ancestors in the Mighty Name of God the Father. After that, you'll say you take this curse and cover it in the Mighty Name of God the Father. You'll repeat that process for the next 12 verses."

"Okay, but how does that work?"

"Well, you've admitted to all your sins and sought His forgiveness and committed your life to Him, so that says you're ready—therefore that honest relationship is so important in getting you on the road to being healed. The rebuke tells Satan or Satan's servant or his curse to leave in the name of God the Father. No matter what others might say, there is no substitute for the word 'rebuke'. Then, by saying the other phrase of the Mighty Name of God the Father, you have the authority of God. So, you're telling Satan to leave, claiming the authority of God and that will wash away the curse and remove it as if it was never there."

We went through the entire process and when it was all over, I took a deep breath, it suddenly felt as if a huge weight had been lifted from my shoulders and all I wanted to do was to smile. When I did that, I got an amazing reaction from Charles.

"Good grief!" he said, laughing himself. "I can't believe this."

"Believe what?" I asked with a goofy grin.

"Go look in the mirror."

I went to the bathroom and saw what he meant. I looked like I was 20 years younger; it was amazing! I looked like a kid because all the junk I carried from my past was lifted from me.

That night, I just called to check in and say hi to Louis, who was eight years old at this time, and I caught him just before bed. I wanted to ask him a few questions about baseball and his schoolwork, but he jumped right in.

"Dad, Dad," he said, "I was in class today and something real funny happened to me."

"Really? What was it?"

"All of a sudden, I had to go to the bathroom really bad, so I went down to the boys' room, when I got there, I didn't have to go, but I was sweating like crazy. I was all wet from sweating!"

I thought that was wild and thanked God that he was okay. I was ecstatic about it but didn't make too much fuss. Once the call had ended, I immediately told Charles and he was just as delighted.

"That was the curse being lifted from your family! You know, it's stopped with you now and your family is no longer cursed. Whatever that generational problem was, it's gone!"

That was an amazing feeling! Knowing that my son would forever be free to live a healthy life. I knew he would still have to make choices yet having the clarity of spirit would give him an inner strength that I didn't think I had when I was growing up.

11

After the final visit to with Charles, I felt so different as I traveled back home. My attitude was so positive! I even thought my marriage could be fixed and we would get over all the problems of the past and look forward to a much more settled future for us and our son. As much as I felt different and even though I looked younger, because of the weight that had been lifted, my wife didn't seem to understand.

"So, how did it go? Are you better now?" she asked after I told her that I would move back in. Her tone clearly suggested that there was never anything wrong with me in the first place and it was all in my head.

"I'm feeling better for sure. It's hard to describe how I feel…"

"But you're all fixed then." Her interruption was clearly a statement, not a question. She left the room, but not before giving me a look that suggested that I had been making everything up, that all our problems were mine and I had better stop causing them in the future. It still seemed that I would be the one blamed if anything went wrong!

I called Charles and told him how she had reacted and I could visualize him shaking his head. He knew my wife quite well, what she was like and that she didn't like him. She could deny what I said, but if someone else backed me up, that put her in a corner, and made it more difficult for her to place all our problems on me. She would get angry with Charles and walk off. She could never believe what she was hearing.

On that call, he reminded me that I was a different person now and I should continue to do my best to save my marriage; I did that for about six more weeks, but things got so bad, I moved out again and went to stay with my mom. I continued to talk to Charles. My wife finally agreed to speak with Charles herself, that seemed to work, and she made some effort. She told me she was changing and even lost some weight to prove it. One day, while I was visiting to get something from the office, we were sitting in our kitchen and talking quite calmly. For the first time in our relationship, she admitted that she might have some problems with intimacy.

"I'm different now so come back," she said and gave me a look that I had not seen in a long, long while.

So, yet again, I did. I thought I would give it another chance, there was even a little bit of excitement for maybe five or six months; some days it was almost like the early days. However, seemingly just as quickly, it turned back to where it had been before, if not worse. I came, with God's help, to realize that it felt like she had simply been manipulating me. There was no marriage as such and my realization and acceptance of that came in a very strange way.

I continued to pray a lot. Late one night I was on my knees in our living room after everyone else was asleep. It felt like I was getting a message to hold my arms out, as I did, I had this sensation that I was holding a body. It was the strangest thing, while I was praying, I was deeply sobbing; I did not really understand what was going on.

The following day was a Sunday. After the service I went for a coffee with a friend who was aware of our situation and had tried to help me in the past. I told him what had happened and for a few moments he just stared out of the window at the people and traffic going by, then he closed his eyes.

"I think I just had ... well, I don't know what to call it except perhaps a revelation," he said after he opened his eyes and turned back to face me.

"Really?"

"I got a little, you know, a little vision," he replied, looking somewhat embarrassed at suggesting such a thing, but then he seemed more confident about what he was saying.

"I think that God was trying to tell you your marriage is dead."

I really didn't know how to react. I believed what he was saying was true, but we had spoken our vows before God so how could we break them irreparably? I went back home and tried to make things work, but that began an even longer cycle over the next year of my moving out and moving back and moving out again.

When I was away from home, I lived at either my mom's or at a friend's condo while he was away on business. I moved to my mom's, moved back, moved to the condo again for a month, moved back. I even took a six-month lease on a place, broke it, and moved back home. I moved to that same place with the six-month lease again, broke it, moved back home, and so it went on until the October 2006.

I finally found a local house for rent and signed a one-year lease which was very expensive and wouldn't be easy to break. I knew this would be a good place to raise my son. It was a few short miles from the marital home and close to my office. So, I slowly started to move some of my belongings there and furnish the house, but I couldn't bring myself to move out permanently because Christmas was close.

By March 2007, two years after I first visited Oklahoma, I had to decide whether to go back home and break another lease or move out permanently. As much as I benefited from my time with Charles, as much as my business was starting to go well, I still lacked confidence and felt insecure. While I knew I had to get up the nerve, I was literally afraid to leave permanently. I knew I just had to decide. The constant moving to and from my marital home was taking a toll on me, but more so, my son. One Saturday morning in early March, while my wife and son were out for the day, I moved out for good.

The final decision came on the back of two incidents, which together showed me it was time to make the break. While still in my marital home, I was sleeping in our spare room on a mattress on the floor. One night, while I was asleep, my wife came in and started spraying me with air freshener, saying that I stunk up the place. Then, around the time we first started seriously talking about a divorce, there was the incident with the stairs.

I walked by her one evening on my way to bed and she said, "Are you trying to push me down the stairs? Did you just try and push me down there?"

"I have never even called you a bad name! You know that, so how could you think that I would ever push you down the stairs?"

That was so scary I hardly slept. The next day I mentioned it to my attorney. He warned me that women sometimes get coached to be able to claim acts of domestic violence to get their husbands into trouble and be forcibly removed from the house. They claim the incident and call the cops and then it looks really bad for the man in court. It could also have led to a restraining order, which would have kept me from seeing my son. That really worried me, so during my final days there I walked on eggshells and was very deliberate about everything I said and did.

That Saturday, as soon as my wife and son were out of the house, I called a friend and we moved many of my belongings. I took my personal items and threw them into bags and boxes, put them into the back of his pickup truck and moved out for good. While the business was doing well, money was still an issue because there were still debts to be paid, but I had to get up the nerve to go.

I was doing better than when I had a job, but now I was going to have to fund two homes. We went to court prior to the divorce proceeding, to determine what type of support I would have to pay.

I had to pay temporary support which was not alimony, so there were no tax benefits; it was just temporary support, or 'pendente lite' as I learned it was called—it wasn't very light to me! Somehow, I managed to come up with the support payments each month. Although I felt this would financially break me, I had to get by and knew I would. This was yet another huge issue to contend with on top of so many others in the past months.

After Oklahoma, I had felt more energized, trying to stay focused on my business and grow my relationship with my son. The divorce process was so intense, it seemed like I was afraid the entire time. "What if I lost everything?" I would think to myself. I had terrible feelings of guilt and shame even though I knew they were unfounded. Relationships were being torn apart like the one with my father-in-law. He is a wonderful man and the divorce process was made even harder because we had such a good relationship. He had always been supportive and positive.

People were choosing sides, friends were either accusing me or supporting me. During the separation and divorce there was so much pressure with the phone calls and meetings with attorneys, as well as the Forensic Accountants digging deep into my financial records. At the same time, I was building my company and hiring people and bringing on new clients, I still spent significant time with my son. I did my utmost to make him feel that he had two real homes where he would be loved, feel safe and nurtured. Doing all that while I felt like I was still falling apart inside was very tough indeed.

When the dust started to settle, I deliberately started making more time for myself. My quiet time was important and much needed. I had been in the habit of praying and reading in the morning, but this was more intentional. I was yearning to have a deeper relationship with God. The first step was finding a good church that could help nurture me spiritually. After visiting a few different churches, I finally found one where I felt accepted and found some new friends that were incredibly supportive.

I felt the need to stop the 'noise' and the constant fast pace, so I scheduled four hours of alone and quiet time one Saturday morning. I knew I would need some fellowship afterwards, so I asked one couple out to dinner to say thank you for being so supportive. That turned into being a rather special day.

In the morning, I removed all distractions—phone, music, computer, and the internet—and locked myself in my house. I sat comfortably in my living room with my arms crossed and said, "Okay Lord, I'm here." I repeatedly said, "Be still and know I Am God." "Be still and know I Am God," until I literally passed out. I woke a little while later feeling much calmer. This softened me to listen and to hear the 'still small voice' inside me. After that I sat, meditated and prayed for hours, asking God about what I needed to do to sort out my life. This huge shift helped me reframe my life and I began a whole number of new and different journeys on my road to healing … and to where I am today.

12

The divorce process began in early 2007, but it dragged on and on. I would still need to pay $6,000 per month until it was all finalized; which wouldn't be until mid-2008. The courts had decided, that this was the amount my ex-wife needed as 'temporary support' to maintain her standard of living—we'd not been paying anywhere near that amount of money when we were together, how could it be this now that we were separated?

It seemed that as far as the court was concerned, it was okay for me to drop my standard of living but not for my soon to be ex-wife. I had no issue, of course, over my son. It was not money he needed, but time and attention!

I managed to handle that amount for many months, but at one point, I just had to cut it down to $4,000 per month because it was starting to crush me. The pressures of having to pay for two homes, my expenses and caring for my son was just too much. In addition, my business was still young and growing and required a lot of capital to keep it moving. I knew the revised amount was enough to cover the mortgage and provide enough for living expenses. My attorney, thank goodness, got her attorney to agree. At that time, my son was in a public school, so that didn't cost additional money, so it was all going to her.

Coping financially was one thing—and the lower payments helped slightly—but I was also learning to cope with what was going on in my head. Because I was still in emotional turmoil, I craved more quiet time. I knew that getting away from the situation was the right thing to do. Looking back, we may have lost everything if we had stayed together. Yet, I still felt terrible guilt and shame that our marriage had failed and that we were about to put our son through all the things that come with a divorce.

Because it had dragged on for so long, there were waves of anger that would hit me, seemingly out of nowhere. I tried to tell myself that Charles had sorted out the issues that I now knew came from my childhood, but that wasn't always the case. The issues like my problems with my self-image continued to add to my overall lack of confidence whenever I stopped to think about them. With all the extra money that I needed, I was spending more time working and growing my business. It seemed as soon as I stopped each day, I often felt like collapsing. My anxiety level over finalizing the divorce was immense and it seemed to drag on like a poorly written soap opera. It just wouldn't go away. All my close friends and family knew about the drama I had faced in my marriage and afterwards—sometimes, I was so upset it was all I could talk about. Every day I felt like I was living on an emotional roller coaster! On top of the stress and drama from the divorce, I was also dealing with all the baggage from my childhood.

I felt emotionally and financially drained, but I was happy to some extent, to be on my own. On the nights when my son wasn't with me, I could find some quiet alone times. When he was with me—he was ten years old when I moved out—I made sure we invested plenty of interactive time together. We had no TV, a deliberate decision, so I wouldn't be lulled into thinking our time together would just be a matter of sitting in front of a screen.

When I first moved to my own place, I remember sitting thinking how to handle all the monthly expenses and thought about how much cable TV would cost. As I considered it, I heard a very quiet voice say, "Sure, go ahead and get a TV so when you come home tired this will be your parenting time!" It scared me to think how easy it would be to push aside the precious time with my son. This was a "God" moment. If the weather was suitable, we would play ball in the yard, go for a bike ride or a walk, but if we remained indoors, we would play wrestle or just have some fun. We would cook and have our meals together. Once his homework was done and after we ate, we would read or play checkers or cards. It was just the two of us with no media or internet to interrupt our night. I did have a laptop with a wireless internet card for my work, but it was rarely taken out during our time together, except for an occasional movie.

For Louis, his mom and I splitting up was hard on him. Even though he seemed to have become accustomed to me moving out and then back home again, it hit him extremely hard when we told him we were getting a divorce. We went to great lengths to show that we still loved him very much and we would both still support him, but it was a tough time for all of us.

For many years after, he had tried pushing us together, even physically trying to drag one of us across the room if we were in the same location. I know he viewed it all as his fault. He felt that because the situation was not normal, and he felt like people would look at him differently. He missed having a family and it hurt me deeply to see him feel that way. Friends and family pointed out how much I tried to save the marriage, but it didn't really lessen the pain and guilt from the way my beloved son felt.

One weekend in May 2007, I was out buying groceries and received a call from someone I had seen for counseling a number of times over the years. His name is Brad, he is about 10 years older than me. He was the pastor of a Christian Church, an author and family man. Brad and I met in the late

1990's through the Amway business. He became my mentor and friend. He was there reassuring me through my divorce and while I was learning to be single again. During this time, I would call him once a week for guidance. His inspiring and reassuring ways helped keep me focused so I didn't go out and "jump off a bridge" and wreck my life. I think of him as my accountability partner. Brad was there for me every week for over 10 years. We still talk today, but now I like to think we support each other.

When we talked, he wanted to know how I was doing, so I ended up going to Starbucks. I bought a coffee and settled into a table by the window. Soon after I sat down, the subject of my son came up.

"He's become kind of distant in school, " I told him. He doesn't engage a lot with other kids or his teachers. I guess, he's just flying under the radar and is skating by on average marks."

"So, had he, you know, seen any of the arguments between the two of you?" he asked, and I shook my head as I responded.

"Not really. As much as it was often spontaneous that we'd get into a disagreement over something, if he came into the room, we would stop but I am sure he could feel the tension.

"So, he never saw how she was behaving or understand what she was putting you through?"

"No, not really. I had been through years of counseling and working on myself to make the marriage work, but he has no idea."

"Do you want to tell him now?" Brad asked, and I looked up sharply.

"No, I can't do that. He wouldn't understand."

"But you would *like* to tell him, to put your side of things down? You would want to do that, wouldn't you … if you could?"

I looked out of the window and all my eyes seemed to focus on were the families. I didn't see the couples or people on their own, just the moms and dads with their kids, laughing and joking and smiling. Once more, I got hit with the guilt like someone had punched me in the stomach, but I knew it wasn't only my fault.

"Yeah, I would ..." I answered quietly.

"Well, I understand, that you don't want to talk about it now, but why don't you go home and write it all down. Don't give it to him yet, that's for when he's older, but write him a letter today. Tell him what happened and how you've been feeling. Get it all off your chest and put it in writing. That is how you're going to help him understand. Believe that eventually, you're going to help him see that you did everything you could to make the marriage work, but in the end, it was doomed to fail, and you had to admit it was over."

"Okay ..." I managed, and he gave me some encouragement.

"Take a copy of the letter and send it through the mail to yourself at your office or new place. Then just keep it sealed until he is 15 or 16 or asks you what happened. You can tell him you did everything you could to keep the marriage together. Then, if the situation calls for it, give him the letter. It will show him that you were concerned for him at the time you captured your feelings. This will help him understand what you were experiencing."

Once again, I was quiet and thought about what he said before I agreed that I would do it, which I later did.

"So how is she behaving now?" asked Brad. "The same?"

"Yeah, there is a lot of animosity, she is still trying to take advantage of me. You know, there was one night just before I left the house, she had been using my computer to do her emails. She was going to bed, but she looked pointedly at me and then at the monitor as if to tell me she'd left her emails open. I was never one to pry, but I did look that one time ..."

"Go on ..."

"Well, she left something open from August two years before we had agreed to anything about the divorce. She had signed herself up on some dating site, Match.com I think. I closed that message and there in the list from that time were other emails from men who wanted to meet her for a date. I looked at the profile she created. The photo she used was from our engagement picture ... but she cut me out."

Brad simply sighed.

"Later on, I found out that it was mutual friends who helped her do it. You know, I thought they were my friends too. In her summary about herself, she said she was a mom who was about to be divorced, but during that time, when I tried to suggest that we end it, she argued with a vengeance that it would never happen."

"Well, that's not for your son, I guess; you only want to state your side of things, but she sure was difficult."

"I can't argue with that," I replied and managed a brief smile. "A week later, we had the same routine, but this time she more pointedly told me to read one of her emails. This was a recent one from a woman who had never met me but had said to my wife that all men have millions stashed away somewhere so she had better find it! There we were, living in debt and surviving from check to check and she thought I was hiding millions of dollars in the bank somewhere!"

"I had the same thing with my ex," said Brad, with a light chuckle.

"Really?"

"Yeah, she was convinced there was lots of money I had been hiding. I know what you mean by that and understand how you feel."

You want to say, 'Aren't you part of this, don't you look at the checkbook?' You just know you would be wasting your time," I replied, and Brad agreed before we said goodbye to each other. After that, I went home and wrote the letter, but never needed to give it to my son. I still have it today, unopened.

Brad knew that I was getting more and more into self-development and the following day, he called me and recommended a book he thought might be helpful. I was able to find a copy in a bookstore later that week. It was titled *The Success Principles*, written by Jack Canfield and it was another catalyst in turning my life around. One key theme of the book is that we are all responsible for our own lives. As I opened the book, there it was on the first page of the first chapter, 'Take 100% responsibility for your life'. That just hit me in a way that I thought to myself, "Wow, I am in the here and now, if I want to get better and if I want to be successful in life, it is up to *me* to take responsibility for my life and it is up to *me* to take care of *me*! It doesn't matter how anyone else acts or what they think or what they say, it's all up to *me*!"

Up to this point, I had developed a habit of rising early, reading, praying, journaling and exercising, but this was more challenging. That line gave me a shift in my thinking. I started studying the book; it is almost 460 pages, and in it Canfield mentions different therapies, Gestalt Therapy, Time Line Therapy, Neuro-Linguistic Programming—NLP, and a process called the Sedona Method. Praying and reading my Bible every morning would always help. I had already been reading personal development books. Most notably; "*Think and Grow Rich*" by Napoleon Hill, "*How to Win Friends and Influence People*" Dale Carnegie, "*Rich Dad Poor Dad*" Robert Kiyosaki, and others listed in the appendix. Now I sought to do something more specifically impactful for myself. I was willing to do whatever I needed to do to grow and overcome the issues of my past. I planted the idea in my mind that I would find someone to help me with whatever theory was relevant for my needs.

I decided that I would begin by finding an NLP practitioner. I hadn't started the process yet when I was having some back issues and was at my chiropractor's office, which was based in a wellness center. While checking out after a visit, I saw a flyer on the counter just looking at me. The flyer promoted a new addition to the practice—a practitioner named Rachel who specialized in NLP. I was really amazed and knew that this could be the person for me.

I learned from the Jack Canfield book that, in simple terms, NLP is an approach to personal development and psychotherapy that was created in the 1970's. The idea is that there is a connection between neurological processes (*neuro-*), language (*linguistic*) and behavioral patterns learned through experience (*programming*) and that these patterns can be changed to achieve specific goals in life. It is suggested that NLP methodologies can help treat problems such as phobias, depression, psychosomatic illnesses and learning disorders. I made an appointment to see her and thus began a fruitful relationship that endures today.

13

I told Rachel about my complicated history and problems. Once that was established, we started working together on a routine basis. In the beginning, we would meet at the wellness center, which was okay for a while. After several months, I started feeling very distracted and noticed that the room was noisy. I was beginning to feel self-conscious and worried that people would think there was something 'wrong' with me. These distractions made it difficult for me to concentrate and feel comfortable. Eventually however, we transitioned to Rachel's office space, which offered a much quieter and calming environment.

The sessions would be an hour and a half to two hours long. My goal was to try to understand what was now going on in my head. I knew I needed to address these things and start to have more control of my thinking and myself. What she told me on that first session is something I still think about today.

"I think your problem is going to be your belief system," she said, smiling across her desk.

"How do you mean?" I asked.

"I'm sure we're going to find that you have a lot of false beliefs, Lou, especially about yourself. Going back to what your uncle had instilled in you at such an early age. I would say that your mind is probably riddled with false and negative beliefs about yourself. Once we find out what those are, we can consider what you might call rewiring and reprogramming those beliefs, so you can get rid of them. Does that make sense?"

"Yeah, it does. This kind of confirms what came out of my

sessions with Charles I really don't seem to trust or respect myself."

"Well, that's true!" she agreed with another smile, "You need to think more highly of yourself. What you need to do, once we've identified the negative beliefs, is to end any other unhealthy relationships in addition to, the one with your ex-wife."

Rachel would ask me questions and based upon my answers she would pose different questions that challenged the beliefs that I never realized were in my head. She would get into my head with these questions to help me loosen up my hold on the old beliefs. What I learned was both amazing and somewhat scary. In short, I had been convinced that I wasn't a very nice person, I didn't deserve to be treated well, and I didn't deserve to be happy. It seemed that all of this came from the abuse that, until recent times, I hadn't even remembered.

However, over time, I started to develop new beliefs and to think more positively about myself. It was a time-consuming, painstaking process, but it was helped by the fact that my spirit was healthier and calmer after Oklahoma. That period with Charles' interventions had offered such a calming effect. Now I got to work on my mental state, my beliefs and my mind itself … and we started to turn things around.

Some of the new beliefs were helping me grow my business. I was becoming more confident about adding new clients and growing what I did for existing ones. I also started believing that I deserved to be paid, paid well and paid on time! After a session where my beliefs around these areas shifted, it seemed like suddenly people would pay me—I was waiting, hoping and praying that these big payments would come in. Amazingly, once I changed my beliefs, within 3 days I would receive a check in the mail that was not due to arrive for another two weeks! I said to myself, you know this stuff really works!

I experienced what you might call a cognitive or mental shift that I deserved to be happy and successful, which meant I was learning to be more accepting of myself. My thinking had been limited and closed-minded. It wasn't healthy for me (or anyone) to be that way. Basically, I had to develop my own values. I did that through the accumulation of my reading, prayer time and now diligently working with Rachel, and using NLP to develop new beliefs. As I let go of the negative beliefs, I had more mental space and began to create some new, positive beliefs about myself and my life.

NLP also helped me benefit more from my quiet time. When Louis was with me, I made sure I was up very early and had my time while he was still sleeping. I found it helpful to concentrate on Proverbs every day when I read my Bible. For a period of three consecutive years I read, studied and meditated on one chapter of Proverbs a day correlating to the date. (I only missed three days in three years). These truths were educating me in the ways of sound wisdom, and I was starting to learn so much more about life.

The Scriptures were very powerful in helping me grow. I felt like I was finally developing a healthy self-image. In addition, my physical and mental health were improving drastically! I was now exercising rigorously five to six days a week, which really picked up when I started working out with Wendy, a high-quality personal trainer. We worked together one day a week. As she trained and challenged me, I was learning how to properly exercise and use *all* my muscles for balance, stabilization, and fitness. I was getting in good physical and mental shape. For me, these daily practices worked together to help me start turning my life around.

My business was moving in an upward direction. My life was getting better, but I was still emotionally up and down. Sometimes it was like a roller coaster ride with the divorce—

one day we were ready to settle and the next day we were going to court again. It still seemed like I was on an emotional rollercoaster and being controlled by outside influences. We were back and forth to court so much that it took its toll despite all the efforts I was making to heal myself. Amid that, I needed to find a new attorney when I realized my existing one felt that, because I was a 'business owner', I could afford to pay an exorbitant weekly alimony for life!

The divorce was finalized 14 months after I moved out of the house for good. In May of 2008; I was relieved of paying the temporary support but still required to pay a hefty sum per week for the next seven years while my son was in school. With the help of my new attorney, I accepted the fact that I didn't deserve to pay for life. Lifetime alimony could have been disabling to my soon to be ex-wife.

She was still young, smart, healthy, well-educated, and could go out and make something of herself if she chose to. If she just sat and collected a check every week for doing nothing, it would kill her spirit. I still wanted her to do well and be happy in life.

Not being saddled with payments in perpetuity helped me understand and accept that I really was starting to climb out of my old life and those old ways. That I, like everyone else in our country, deserved the freedoms we are privileged to enjoy.

On the day the divorce was finalized, I was at the court early, far too early, in fact. I have no idea why I went there so much earlier than I needed to, but I guess I was so nervous about having a judge decide my financial future that I wanted to make sure I was prepared. Prior to that day, my attorney had tried to reassure me, but he could never really predict the outcome and couldn't get a good read on the judge. When I arrived in court, my attorney was meeting with my wife's attorney. My wife wasn't around either. It was very quiet, the courtroom itself was locked and I sat alone outside the courtroom in the waiting area. I was on my own for a long time, for over an hour just waiting, pacing, praying and trying to stay calm. I thought I was going to go crazy. Then I went for a walk around and found a painting that caught my eye.

The courthouse is in an historic town where General George Washington stayed and fought with his troops during the Revolutionary War. In tribute to him was a painting of George Washington as our first President. I had read about Washington and his life, as I stared at the picture, I said to him, "If you can go through what you did and live, I can go through this and live."

I realized while standing there that everyone, including successful or prominent people, must go through adversity and trying times. Not only do they come through it, but they go on to live productive, meaningful and even significant lives. As I continued my walk, I decided positive thinking was part of releasing those old, negative beliefs, achieved from my work with Rachel. It calmed me and really helped me develop the resolve to accept and overcome whatever the judge's decision was and move on with my life.

Eventually, we all entered the courtroom, and gave our testimony. Of course, my wife's attorney tried to discredit me, but my attorney really went all out for me. I believe one reason for this was; the day I found out that most attorneys only partially believe their clients because we all interpret things differently. That day we were discussing parenting time when my attorney asked, "Mr. Samara how many hours a week do you spend time with your son?" I replied by opening my planner and counted the times I was with him. The nights he spent with me, the school functions and ball games I attended etc. Then he said, "You're for real, aren't you?" I didn't understand the question. He explained that most people just say they spend a lot of time with their children. They don't know how much time but generally overestimate. I showed him how much time and from then on, he felt he could trust my word and really went to bat for me. To this day he remains a trusted advisor and we have become good friends!

We negotiated the terms and the judge agreed. The judge gave me seven years of costly alimony however, a big win for me was I didn't have to pay for her legal fees. Additionally, prior to our son starting High School—the original family house was to be sold. Once the sale was completed, we were to split the equity and move forward.

I was relieved when the day was over, and the ordeal finally finished. Although I would only be paying limited alimony and my legal fees, I still had the feeling that I was taken advantage of. I wondered if this is how most people feel after finalizing a divorce. I decided at that moment, I would move forward, continue to take care of my son, myself and pay the support while rebuilding my life.

14

If you asked me to consider working with someone like Rachel when I was a SWAT officer, I probably would have flippantly laughed at the idea! What had moved me to start using her services now and why was I was continuing with the sessions? I considered this question in some detail one morning when I was stuck in traffic after a truck had hit a bridge. I thought about how I was feeling, which was a combination of being scared and excited. I knew I was growing and wanted to explore more to get healthier, but I was concerned what I might unearth.

When I first met Rachel, she was already a master NLP practitioner, yet was continually looking to progress and implement new practices. I guess that's why we worked so well together; we both like to constantly grow and evolve. As she sought to improve her skills, I was a 'beneficiary' of the advances she made in her client offerings. During my time working with her I also sought other help. I had business mentors and coaches, financial, tax and legal advisors as well as two chiropractors who practiced holistic medicine and nutrition. I was part of a weekly men's group and had a spiritual mentor who was a pastor of a Christian church and counselor. With all this emotional processing occurring in me I found respite in massage, acupuncture, reiki energy therapy and a host of other techniques which helped me stay on my healing path.

Rachel helped identify where my emotional challenges were originating. She employed many different methods, even blending them, to help me continue to heal, grow and to release all the old unhealthy emotions inside me. As we discussed this one day, we equated my progress to an educational program.

I had started on this journey of self-inquiry and looking inside to try to understand why I felt certain ways. I wanted to be free from all the horrific memories that were churning in my brain and the negative emotions that haunted me daily. I started to look at successful people and say to myself, "Well, if they can be successful, then why can't I?" There was no reason why I couldn't!

I learned so much from being in the Amway business, the successful people associated with Amway and most importantly, their training systems. As I started to develop some control of my emotions and improved my skills for better relationships, I realized something was still holding me back. I started to think about Jack Canfield, not about him as the author of the book that had become so important to me, but about him as a person; he was just like me. Here was a very successful man who went through some real growth as he spent time on NLP, Gestalt and Time Line therapies. Was he a better person than me? No, so why not me?

I decided to see what would happen, if I really started to question things for myself. I became more inquisitive and tested my beliefs and actions. Why did I feel this way? Why do I act that way? Why did I believe certain things? I also considered why I felt I couldn't get ahead in life and why I was living in mediocrity even though I had big dreams. I wanted to accomplish great things and make a difference in the world. I wanted to make an impact, and felt I wasn't. I knew I needed to do more!

When I started working with Rachel, that's where I was. I admit that those initial sessions were emotionally painful, but I came through each of them better and stronger. For me to open up as much as I needed to, I had to trust God, trust her, trust myself and trust the process. I found that, deep down, I really didn't totally trust anyone; including myself. I was still carrying around, on a deeper level, a lot of fear, terror, anger, sadness, shame, and guilt. I was feeling these emotions at different times. Most of the time, I felt extremely guilty.

Here's a very real and almost embarrassing example of how the guilt and shame affected me in my daily life. What I found, while working with Rachel, was very interesting and freeing. From my early childhood and into the early stages of having my own business, anytime—and I mean anytime—someone called me by my first name, I thought I was in trouble. They would just have to say my name and immediately, without ever considering who it was or what the circumstances where I would think, "Uh-oh, here it comes. I'm in trouble." It was a huge load to carry. I felt better when they didn't use my name. That's how guilty I felt from all the abuse in my early childhood. Imagine what insecurities those incidents perpetuated for most of my life.

I also felt a fear of being vulnerable and a fear of being weak, like I had to be in control of everything to feel safe. I always had to look good; I always had to be perfect. I had to be liked, to be successful and to make sure everything was in place, so I looked great. Whew!! What a *huge* burden to carry, and what a wholly unsustainable standard to live up to. At some level this was exhausting! It was no wonder that I was emotionally drained! All of this was holding me back from being the *real* me! It seemed I was continually battling against those negative emotions to an extent where it was hard for me to feel anything except guilt.

Yet as I progressed, I started to open up and began to trust Rachel *and* to trust myself. I always knew I could trust in God on certain levels, but deep down in my emotions, there was a big fear about this too. This was tied in with the guilt that I carried, I felt like I was going to do something wrong. I thought that even God was going to hate me or that He was going to hurt me if I did something wrong.

One of the biggest hurdles for me was to get past all the unconscious anger towards the people in my past who, like my uncle and grandmother, had hurt me. Yet, as I was surfacing and addressing my problems, I was still struggling not to point the finger of blame at myself. I also didn't want to hurt other people. Instead of lashing out at people or calling them bad names or demeaning them, I would keep it inside. . I would bury it and direct it towards myself. I was so sensitive, I couldn't calmly communicate my feelings or thoughts and always felt like I was on the defensive.

I came to understand that I really had to learn to love myself! One thing that seems both funny and sad now is that I had to teach myself to smile at the thought of *me*. I learned to look in the mirror and say to myself "I love you." In the beginning, the first few times I tried, it was the weirdest thing. After staring at my reflection for a while, I looked in the bathroom mirror and as sincerely as I could, I said, "I love you, Lou." And something changed.

It was not just from saying it, but I felt kind of weird, so I started to repeat that over and over during the day. I started to reinforce it as a true belief, which was the first step in breaking through some of the barriers of self-hatred. I had to treat myself better, which was not only saying "I love you," but by lovingly caring for myself.

As I continued to work with Rachel, I was still engrossed in the study, application, and re-reads of numerous books. I became a voracious reader. At the forefront was The Bible, but also, I repeatedly devoured *The Success Principles, Think and Grow Rich, The Magic of Thinking Big,* and numerous other books that I felt were particularly appropriate for my situation and life. I had to learn not to let the titles of these books sway or intimidate me and accept they were written to help me understand myself and others and how to interact successfully with people.

I was understandably nervous and a little skeptical about what I might get—or not—from the NLP sessions. As I saw how positive the sessions and teachings from those books were. I opened my mind and became willing to look at different methods and approaches. Which in the end, were all different ways of healing for me. I was very concerned to make sure I stayed on a good spiritual path, which I saw as my true foundation. I didn't want to get persuaded into some type of brainwashing that may exist with some extreme cults and accepted there was no danger of that. Also, in reading Proverbs and developing discernment, I found I could make better decisions on which programs I chose. Those books and Rachel herself assured me that whatever avenue I explored next, would be beneficial to my healing.

I knew that the authors I liked had solid values, were believers in God and with a strong faith. So, if they recommended something and I was satisfied with my research, I was going to be happy with that. Most of these healing methodologies like Gestalt Therapy and Time Line Therapy, as well as NLP were foreign to me. I made a conscious decision to try these methods because of the success and benefits that Canfield and others had experienced going through these therapeutic methods. He also mentioned something called the Sedona method developed by a man named Hale Dwoskin. So, I ordered the set of CDs' and started to study along with the accompanying book.

The Sedona Method is designed to show you how to uncover your natural ability to let go of any painful or unwanted feelings. It consists of a series of questions you ask yourself that lead your awareness of what you are feeling in the moment and gently guide you into the experience of letting go. The Sedona Method is based on the power of feelings—if you *feel* powerful, then you act powerfully. If you feel sad, then you act sadly. Dwoskin tells us that our feelings define how we operate in the world and unless we change those feelings—when they are negative influences—we are going to act as we have always acted, and we will produce the 'results' we've always produced. As much as there are different teachings on this subject, some say you act your way into feeling-which as a base works very well. I thought because of all my suppressed feelings I would combine this approach with my daily routine.

My office was about a five-minute walk from my house, so when I got the set of CD's I would come home for lunch several days a week then sit and listen to them to go through whatever process it required. I did that for several months and continued to spend time doing NLP sessions with Rachel. Along with my daily routine quiet time, study time, self-talk and listening to positive audios, these approaches kept me moving forward until I realized I was getting healthier in my mind and the negative beliefs were changing. At times however, it was still a *real* struggle.

15

Even though it seemed that I might have been outwardly positive, on the inside I found I was sabotaging myself. My mind seemed to be programmed that way and it was very difficult to totally break free of those old beliefs. I had to fight what I kept hearing in my subconscious, that I was 'worthless'. I would get a real emotional boost from my time working with Rachel or from some of my quiet time. Then for no reason, I would find myself feeling down again, living with those repeating cycles of feeling like a constant failure.

I talked to Rachel about this and she decided to start using a mix of varying therapies that included NLP and Time Line Therapy (TLT). She asked me if I understood what it was all about, I told her that I had read some things but asked her how she thought it would be useful relating to me and my issues.

"Okay, here you go. I have found that Time Line Therapy is a pretty powerful therapeutic process. It's evolved from hypnosis and NLP and was developed by a man named Tad James in the 1980s. It works on the concept that we store our memories in a linear manner in our internal memory storage system. It's proven to help a great deal in supporting what you might call personal change and growth by facilitating the elimination of the painful emotions attached to memories or events in the past. Make sense in your case?"

I nodded, feeling some excitement, but still mostly trepidation.

"TLT, as it's referred to, also focuses on what we can learn from those events, no matter how horrific and use what we learn as a resource for the future. The techniques and practical processes can produce long-lasting transformation much quicker than other methods believe me when I tell you this Lou, there is minimal discomfort to the client. OK?"

"Go on."

"TLT can help you clear those limiting beliefs that are keeping you stuck in the past and are stopping you from creating what you truly want in your life. It can enable someone to release whole chains of emotions rather than one at a time. If the person has anger issues, TLT can facilitate the releasing and clearing of all anger from the past and not just the anger attached to a particular event."

"Well, that sure sounds like it might be good for me," I admitted. "Anything else?"

"Honestly, I think it will be. I wouldn't even go there if I thought it would be wasting your time. The anger is released from what you might call its roots and I believe that this is one of the main reasons why many people are able to get the result they want so quickly. This is really important for you Lou because I know you feel you keep slipping backwards, unable to experience lasting results."

"But this is not about trying to get rid of the memories, right? I can't see that working." I said.

"No, it's not, so don't think that the memories of those painful events will be gone, it's only the negative emotions attached to the memories that we can act upon. Memories are our history and it is not appropriate to clear them."

"Alright," I said, now starting to feel I was getting a good grasp, beyond what I had read, of how this methodology might relate to and help me.

"TLT is invaluable in enabling individuals to resolve negative emotional issues from the past and clear limiting beliefs and decisions that may have prevented them from moving forward and achieving their goals for the future. That's why this is so 'you', Lou because reading about TLT would mean you'll see examples of limiting beliefs such as, "I don't deserve it" or "I am just not good enough" or …"

"You want me to give you a longer list?" I interrupted, and we both laughed together for the first time in a while. From the nod of her head that came at the same time, I felt that Rachel was pleased that I was making some progress.

Rachel asked me to get settled in my chair and began to talk to me.

"Okay, what are you feeling? What do you want to discuss or talk about?"

I asked my mind what it was focusing on and immediately came up with the answer. I wanted to address my terrible feelings of guilt.

"Okay, just close your eyes and picture yourself out in the universe, high above the earth and you're looking down at some incident from your past. Just pick one, but don't get into the situation. You are not in that situation but looking down at it."

Knowing that, I picked an incident that occurred with my uncle. Rachel asked me to describe what I was seeing and feeling. We then worked through a series of questions until I could see that who I truly am was not how I described myself. That belief was captured from that specific moment in time, from that incident and I believed it as truth. I would look at my spirit, my 'true' self and see that the boy in the image was no longer me. It never truly was, but I had accepted it as so.

I started to feel real progress from these sessions and as Rachel continued to challenge me, I was learning that once clear of them, I could never go back to those old beliefs. It seemed like they were now 'scrambled' and as hard as I tried (I tested this many times), I couldn't recall those old limiting beliefs. Once we came out of a session, I could see that my old perceptions were wrong and full of false beliefs. Even without my looking at the scenes of the abuse, I found I could argue against my old perceptions of myself.

"Okay, what are your beliefs now?" she asked one evening. "List them and I'll write them down."

"I believe I'm free. I believe I'm strong, I believe I'm pure and whole and healthy," I replied almost immediately and now I laughed out loud. "Where did all that come from?"

"Those are your beliefs, Lou. These are your new beliefs because those old beliefs weren't even yours to begin with, yet you took them on."

We spent quite a while embracing these new beliefs and they just kept coming. When I got home from work the next day, I read an email that Rachel sent me. The email had a list attached of what I had said about my new beliefs. I still have that email today because its messages remain so powerfully impactful.

Subject: Your Positive Learnings
Date: Wednesday, February 25, 2009 2:30 PM
From: Rachel@xxx.com
To: LSamara@xxx.com

Hi Lou

Before I give you the first set of positive learnings from yesterday, I need to tell you a few important things. At the end of the session you were feeling naturally tired, so I just touched on the topic of tasking. In order for your change to really stick you need to do your tasks as these reinforce all the work that we completed so successfully.

In your quiet time every day I want you to focus on asking yourself "who am I?" and "what is my essence?" Some days it will be beneficial to focus on your strongest positive learnings, get in the state of "acting as if" and enjoy the positive feelings surrounding that learning.

Buy a journal and write every day. Let the words that you write speak of your positive learnings and personal growth. Always remember to keep it with you help you to keep focusing on what you want in life—in every area of your life.

A considerable amount of your energy has now been freed up from old issues that used to restrict you in some way. You are now free to charge ahead with all your goals for the future, putting your energy into what you want.

Keep reminding yourself about the cause and effect relationship, especially leading up to and during conversations with others—remember that we can only perceive in others what exists in ourselves. Well-meaning friends and family may find that your new behavior unsettles them in some way. Remember that they have known the 'old Lou' for a long time. Be gentle yet firm with them, be true to yourself and honor your changes. I suggest that you carefully consider your response to anyone who makes comments about how you are now.

Keep bending the rules and make time for yourself ...

See you soon,

Rachel

Rachel attached a list of the positive learnings I had espoused that ran to four pages! She marked in bold some of those that had seemed to have a lot of energy for me. Here is a selection of the most meaningful and powerful:

I love myself
I am forgiven
I am healed
I am released
I can choose
I am timeless
I am pure
I am everlasting
I can trust myself
I will always be safe
I am protected
I can be myself
I am only responsible for me
I am worthy
I have a choice
I have been set free

Needless to say, all of those words helped a lot and seemed to bring an element of healing to my own heart.

16

As I undertook further sessions with Rachel, I continued listening to the Sedona CD's. At that time, they remained useful. What this was doing was enabling me to 'feel' my feelings. What I learned from listening and working with Rachel was; by suppressing my true feelings I couldn't fully experience the healthy ones. If I was mad or hurt or upset or distraught, the 'old me' just suppressed those feelings. I would never allow myself to let the bad feelings out thus, I would internalize all the unhealthy emotion. This practice was negatively affecting my health.

As I started to treat myself better, I would feel the emotions and let them go. I learned to think differently and if someone said something I didn't like, so what? I couldn't control what they said. I learned that I had to change my 'self-talk' (what I was saying to myself), so equally, I would have to change my response to other people and learn to be more accepting. What I found of most value in doing this, was I learned to accept myself. What a refreshing relief!!

It was always easier for me to accept other people and their issues. While the acceptance of 'myself' was hard and I had a huge learning curve. I finally learned to open myself up to who I am, as well as, to acknowledge what happened in my life. I also learned to agree that, no matter how hard I tried or what image I portrayed, I am not perfect and could never be. I've made mistakes and poor choices along the way, yet, everything added up to who I am, and where I am, which is just part of my life.

The negative events were part of my life and something that happened which was out of my control, I realized I could let go of those feelings and build a positive life. I started to create healthy encounters like spending more purposeful time with my son. I wanted to create more meaningful experiences and better memories. I hoped we would do more together, as a father and son and have a base, so our relationship would continue to flourish. One of these experiences was when I started teaching him how to drive at the age of 12! The first time was in our driveway where I showed him the basics and allowed him to move the car about 10 feet. Then later we went to a quiet corner in a huge parking lot, I drove him around then asked if he wanted to give it a try.

"What! Can I actually do that?" he asked, and I nodded.

"Sure, if you want to."

"But like … you mean me drive the car?"

"Sure. We swap places and you drive."

"Oh wow, Dad! That's just so cool!"

It was so exciting for both of us and he loved it! I poured a lot of time into him and into myself, time with God, time to pray, to sit and reflect, time studying, time reading. After my mentors' first suggestion of a journal, I would make notes in books, I would record things in journals, write them down on the back of envelopes, whatever came to me I wanted to be sure to capture that moment and not lose it. Prior to the journal recommendation I used (and still use although not as many) 3" x 5" note cards and carried them around with me, reading and studying what I had written. It all helped.

Once I started to really understand and 'feel' my feelings, I recognized that emotions come and go like waves in the ocean. They come and go. Let that wave wash through you instead of trying to stop it. It took me a long time to stop putting up a wall or try capturing the wave, pushing it down inside and keeping it there. That's what I had done most of my life. I kept stifling all those negative or fearful emotions and pushing them down because I didn't know how to handle them. Candidly, I didn't think I could feel those emotions.

Before, I could be angry, but I wouldn't show it and did my best not to feel it. But now, I learned that accepting 'feelings' then letting them wash over me was okay and that there is a difference between when you 'feel the feeling', or stuff it down or actively try to push it away. This new way was very different from, the complete opposite, of how I learned to cope as child … which I hadn't changed for over 40 years.

Around the time I started with Rachel, someone asked me why I was so sensitive—I reacted and immediately responded that I was not sensitive! Acting like they poked me in the face! I realized that I wasn't sensitive, I was just very defensive. It was ingrained in me as a kid to make sure I looked good for other people. I was taught that what others thought of me always mattered and this was repeated over and over so I had to be someone that was different than the real me. This wasn't about my true self-image, it was about what I sought to portray to others. My self-image, which was troubling for me, wasn't always who I appeared to be.

I had to learn to become free enough to be my true self. I have worked very hard to get to this point. Right now, I can be angry with people, but I pause before responding and calm myself, so we can work through the issue. Before I would have been mad and offended then bury my emotions because I wanted them to like me. I couldn't think clearly enough to say, "I disagree" or "Would you explain the reason you did this or that?" or "I feel angry about what you did but let's work through this together."

I have found that we never really know what issues someone else is facing that may have caused him or her to act the way they did. An explanation can diffuse a situation, and even save a relationship!

No one ever worried about how I was feeling inside, which

was one of my biggest challenges. I didn't know how to demonstrate what or how I was feeling because I was so afraid from all the abuse I endured as a child. I was afraid I would be physically hurt if I disagreed or explained my feelings. If I felt something negative, I tended to ignore it because I felt wrong, bad, guilty, or shameful; now, I can deal with all of that. The person I am today is most certainly not the one who started working with Charles.

Back then, I tried to be perfect all the time. We still joke about it, today, when we work together. In those early days, I was building my company and those sessions along with prayer, the books, audios, and quiet time, helped me with my mindset and how to remember I am human and will make mistakes. I also had business coaches, advisors, and mentors in all areas of my life, which helped me to see life from different viewpoints. Along with live coaches, I include the Bible, books, audios, and seminars as part of my mentors. So, if you don't have a mentor pick up a book I've mentioned and dig in. Then start asking for guidance from people who are in a place you want to be. When you choose a mentor be sure to look at the whole picture. Everyone has adversity, look at how your potential mentor handles that adversity. Make sure they have the morals and values you seek.

As my company grew, the clarity of mind along with mentoring, helped me improve my attention to detail and to become a critical thinker. As I let go of the negatives, I had more room in my head to think. There was a lot less emotional noise! My mentors held me accountable and led me to strive for excellence, to strive to be better, to grow and think through a process to resolve a problem instead of just reacting to it.

I also learned to respond to situations very differently than I had in my past. Instead of immediately bottling up the emotion of anger, I could now take a breath and tell myself it was no big deal as I got to the heart of the problem. I got past the sensitivity of worrying compulsively, if someone didn't like me. I thought it was necessary to fix the issue immediately. Now I recognize that not everybody is going to care about or like me; it's just human nature. I also learned to appreciate when others vehemently disagree with me, it's not about me but about their viewpoint. Now, I see that's a good thing. We can all learn from each other.

As I learned to understand and live with my new way of thinking, I started to clear my mind of unwanted emotions, thus having more 'space' in my head. Now I could handle the issues; I was gaining more emotional strength and fortitude to raise my son, have healthy relationships and grow a company. With that clear space in my mind, I could be calm, creative, solve problems and come up with answers, more quickly. I realized, when you can feel or experience the feelings, and emotions fully, they can be processed more easily and you can better handle the important things in life.

Another of the lessons I learned is to stop being so hard on myself and to stop suppressing. I learned to feel the anger of those old suppressed feelings, throughout my entire body, in my whole system and then let it go. It was all so very different for me. I felt physically better when I stopped holding on to those unhealthy emotions deep inside my body. I've had digestive issues most of my life because I was internalizing all those ill feelings. Now things are much better.

While I have come a long way, I remind myself this is a lifetime journey. I understand that it's okay and necessary to experience and express feelings of anger or hurt; to be upset and cry. I work to accept them throughout my body, mind and spirit. It is also part of continuing to build a strong relationship with Louis, to ensure that I have the mental capacity and energy to do that while being a patient, loving, encouraging, available and consistent father.

The more I have 'healed', the more the relationship with him has grown and improved. As we spent time together, we made it quality time, building a healthy foundation for our relationship. He knew I loved him and would always be there for him. As with the business, I now had the mental space to be patient and creative, to think and take responsibility as I sought to nurture him and help his development.

My improved sense of 'self', my identity, also helped me understand that when my clients paid me a lot of money for a service, I was responsible for making sure they received everything they paid for... and more! If I sent an employee, they would also be responsible, but I would ultimately have the final responsibility. It allowed me to mature the business, yet there was a kind of dual purpose because the business was maturing me.

There was a time, on two separate occasions when two of my clients got mad at a situation and criticized me in front of others. This was really embarrassing and even hurtful, but while I was upset, I didn't lash back at them and I didn't internalize it. We made a mistake. I accepted it and acknowledged it. It's okay, I reassured myself. We'll work through it, I reassured them.

As I let go of the negative emotions and discovered more emotional stability, I was having more success, and I was growing stronger, tougher, and becoming more resilient. I was more authentic and patient. Well...I'm still working on the patience part! Even though I was already an adult for many years, I needed to become more mature and as I did, I was more confident and much more creative. As I let go of those toxic emotions. I had more mental capacity to create solutions in life and in my business.

We developed unique service programs, business processes and systems which became so successful that a public entity eventually sought out and purchased my company. I wasn't sitting there wondering why I was tired and trying to drown my sorrows in whatever; there was more room for me to focus my energy on what was important in my life.

During this time, I was still attending Amway conferences, which had a very positive and uplifting environment. I also remained very involved in attending my church. Staying in positive environments was helping me, plus my home was calm; it was just my son and me with no TV. I continued building on my habits of quiet time, reading, praying, meditating, studying and exercising. I know you've heard me say it many times throughout this book so forgive me ☺ for constantly repeating this...It's so important for you to develop a process for creating peace and calm in your life. For you, your family and all of us, I hope you find a way to do it!

When I needed it, I would have a session with Rachel and she would help me look, from up in the universe, back down on past events in my life, to continue to work on those emotions and feelings. I don't believe in past lives as such and didn't get too worried by my family heritage and the curse that Charles revealed, but because I trusted in the process going back in time to review those terrible experiences became wonderful healing opportunities. It was out of those that I began to learn to forgive.

17

As a master NLP practitioner, Rachel researched and implemented new techniques and skills to grow her practice. As she sought to improve her skills, I was a beneficiary of the advances she made in her client offerings.

She would mix different approaches together as appropriate. If I went too deep into the scene of an emotion it could be too much and I could get stuck or become overwhelmed with negative emotion. Rachel would have me visualize myself above it all, as I had in time-line therapy. I became quite adept at it and in my mind, could put myself out in the middle of the universe, with the earth beneath me, the sun behind and above me. I would sit there think about my life and pick a point from my past experiences. She would ask me what I was feeling and allow me to guide my own process and be there to keep it moving forward.

She asked me what I was feeling, wanted to address or where I wanted to go. Then my subconscious would pick an incident or I would say I wanted to explore a certain emotion. With that, I could end up in a scene from a long time ago. I wasn't always sure about the exact timing, but it was part of something that happened to me that I needed to learn from and then release.

Sometimes when I visited a scene, it seemed like the incident had happened to someone in my family. No matter what it was, I just went into the scene, felt the emotion, and learned the lesson from it. Once I learned my new belief, I could let it go and stop trying to over-analyze the exact specifics and find out why it was in my subconscious mind. I just allowed my spirit and The Lord's presence to lead me.

In one event, I was enslaved to a man in an animal skin outfit. I was in bondage, trapped and afraid. I was in the story and emotion of the scene.

"Okay," said Rachel, "I want you to come above and look down at the incident. Tell me what's going on and what you are feeling right now."

"Well, it feels like he is beating me. I am trying to get free, but he's keeping me in bondage."

"Have you tried to get away?"

"I have, but I can't. I'm in chains and very afraid. I have a strong feeling that I'm trapped and my life is hopeless."

"Okay, you're getting too close to the scene. Come up a bit and stay above it. Just float above and look down at the scene. Now what are you seeing?"

"It's changing now, and I don't recognize the man in the animal skin. His face is not defined. He won't let me go ..."

Rachel worked through a series of questions, taking me through that incident which helped me realize that it was something that happened as part of my Time Line Therapy. I accepted that I was not in bondage to that person, event, memory, or emotion. I understood that what happened was somewhere in my mind and it was just an old event that was no longer valid in my life. I no longer needed to feel that fear or feel that hopelessness in my life because whatever it was, whatever had happened, I released it and it was over. To this day, I don't really understand what I was remembering—it might relate to some version of being hung on the chains in the basement or it may be the way my mind processed my feelings from the abuse, but it was no longer a factor in my life.

After facing these events from my past, I needed quiet time to let things process and to assimilate the change in my life, so I could practice my new beliefs. After most sessions, I felt a huge shift or release of energy that had been tied up from years of suppressed emotions. I would feel more energetic, happy and relieved. There were times however, I would need more rest the next day or so because my body was still processing the change.

It was important to take time to process this physically, as a result, I had more peace and clarity of mind. The increased energy and newfound joy lasted three to four weeks, sometimes longer, before I was ready for another session.

While I was learning how to experience my emotions and move on from my past to live life, I found it was still difficult to develop the habit of letting go. Although I was learning to process my feelings, I still let the stresses of life build up. I would get entangled in the mix between being a good parent, the divorce process, exercising, a good diet and building a company. By creating additional pressures from my own negative self-talk, I would find myself feeling drained, angry, hopeless, or worthless. In all of this, I was diligent with my morning routines and when I needed to, I would call Rachel or another advisor to schedule a session.

By taking more responsibility for my own development and healing, I extended the time between needing a session, yet I still seemed to be waiting until my next session to resolve issues. This led me to fall into the cycle of needing the next one. When I finally admitted I was addicted to fixing myself, the bubble of the necessity to find something to blame; for where I was or how I was feeling, burst. I was simply me. I was getting more and more into a position where I could either help myself or learn to handle my emotions without assistance.

Along with my morning routines, I devoured books like *Who Switched off My Brain?* by Dr. Caroline Leaf. In her book she shares research, which shows that 87% to 95% of mental and physical illnesses are a direct result of what she calls 'toxic thinking'—proof that our thoughts affect us physically and emotionally. In this best-selling book, she communicates a number of ways to detox your thoughts and live a life of physical, mental, and emotional wholeness.

I have created a positive living environment in my home. I listen to uplifting, motivating music and exercise five or six days a week. Around the house, we have posted positive sayings and verses of scripture, along with pictures of inspirational people like Joan of Arc, Dr. Martin Luther King Jr., Henry Ford, Jesus Christ, President George Washington, Michael Jordan and others. Please know that these sayings have graduated from handwritten notes and word document printouts taped and pinned on a wall to a framed and more polished look, as permitted by my wife! On my desk is a digital frame with pictures of goals and people who I have a goal to associate with. Creating this environment keeps my mind focused on positive thoughts and outcomes. Rigorous exercise keeps my blood circulating, gets my mind in gear and my keeps body cleansed of toxins. I eat well, drink lots of water, and only a little wine!

In an effort to sustain my growth, I created a supportive network for myself. I learned to employ the habits of people who are successful in life, not just business. I planned my days, so I could accomplish the goals I set for myself in order to keep moving forward. It wasn't a perfect routine and I didn't do everything every day, but I always had my quiet time.

I found a church that was the 'right fit' for me with a sound statement of faith. I was welcomed, felt joy and love and learned from the message. One of the Pastors asked me to help lead a men's group, which I did for over four years. The comradery was good, and I was able to teach what I was learning about personal development and letting go!

I also had a great support team with Amway. A little-known secret about this business is the team. We developed many good friendships, some of which have endured over 20 years.

We were all there for each other and knew what we stood for in our lives with our shared hopes and goals of a better future.

My minor success with the Amway business brought me some national recognition, which eventually led to me being asked to speak at conferences. This was another huge boost and builder of my confidence. When I spoke at those events, I typically covered basic skills in business and self-development, but it seemed that people were inspired by my talks because of the challenges I had overcome.

I think they saw that I was just a regular person like them. I came from nothing and was starting to experience success in my life. I was happy to be around people who loved and were loved by their family and I enjoyed being around people with solid values. The Amway business team supported me in these areas.

Being part of that 'business family' helped shape my life and gave me some good fundamentals, but it also helped me learn how to make better choices. I learned to pause and look ahead before I decided. What do I choose to do with my son? Do I choose to go to a movie or play basketball? What will have a better impact for him? Do I choose to take him for ice cream just to spend time with him or leave him in front of a TV or computer screen? Do I choose to invest time in our relationship now or when it's too late? I chose time and activities with him that were value-based and had redeeming qualities for our future.

I realized that I was the author of my life and I needed to choose wisely. Every day was mine to choose what I did and that, I believe, was my biggest driver in all of this. I wanted freedom to choose what I wanted for my life … now I can. Gone are the limiting beliefs that made me feel like I had no choice. For so long, I felt like I had no choices and just had to 'go with the flow' or do what everyone else does; I felt like I was trapped.

Prior to my work with Charles and Rachel, it felt like I wasn't allowed to have a choice, and maybe this came from that image of me being in bondage or a slave, but after my work with them, life was so different.

With the Amway opportunity, everyone is an independent business owner. My job was to introduce a person to the Amway business. I would help them create an income by marketing quality products and referring others. Amway would pay leadership bonuses based upon the volume of product sales and how we helped our customers solve a problem by using our products. It was a win-win situation; the more people we helped the more volume we produced. The more volume we produced, the more we earned. With its specific model and strong team approach, the marketing structure worked very well. That opportunity meant additional financial success. I am extremely grateful for the professional development program and how it helps its members thrive.

18

For over twenty years, I have studied the principles of the Bible, self-development, personal improvement and success. I have experienced many different therapies along with a considerable amount of counseling and coaching. During this time, I've learned to form my own beliefs, opinions and ideas based upon what worked for others and the relevance of my own experiences.

I have considered how my sessions with Rachel were conducted and unfolded. In the beginning when I was first learning to trust myself, Rachel was there to facilitate. I started to progress and understand how much they were 'Spirit-led'. When I went into a session, I would pray and ask the Lord to guide the process. I didn't worry about Rachel controlling or leading me astray. This was more about tapping into the internal me or my subconscious mind. Our mutual trust grew over time. This wasn't her saying, "You must do this," but more my inner self, leading to where I needed to go so, I would be healed. Because I had studied similar types of fundamentals from reading *Think and Grow Rich* by Napoleon Hill, and a few other trusted books these sessions didn't seem unusual.

Rachel and I developed a process to assess where I was on the day of the session. Some days she would do Reiki (a Japanese technique for stress reduction and relaxation that also promotes healing) energy work depending on what I needed most at the time. Most times, we let the spirit lead, with my subconscious mind identifying the hurt that needed to be addressed. After each session, we would talk a little bit about what was going on. Following one Reiki session, Rachel said something that was a trigger to help me really move forward.

"You know, during our session, I found a cage in your chest, around your heart."

"How do you mean? I'm not sure I understand," I asked, sitting forward in my chair and resting my elbows on my knees.

"I didn't tell you at the time, but you're ready now. I'm talking energetically and it's like a barrier. Your heart was locked inside—your heart was locked up—it was like the cage was protecting your heart, so you would not be hurt again. Now the cage is removed and as you've progressed, you learned to trust the process and trust yourself. We've made good progress, by using your energy in healthier ways now, so I think we're ready."

"Ready for what?"

"To begin what I might call your *true* journey to being well. To begin the journey of forgiveness. We're going to work on two different journeys—a physical one and an emotional one. What we are going to do aligns with a book called *The Journey* by a woman named Brandon Bays. This book is all about finding direct access to the soul and unleashing its potent powers to heal."

I was quite stunned by this idea, but if Rachel said it was right for me, then I was okay with that. Because I had learned to trust our process, I still haven't read the book but told her I was ready and made my next appointment.

We started with a physical journey and I was directed to sit and start breathing deeply as Rachel used some relaxation techniques to help me relax.

"Picture yourself walking down a beautiful staircase, every time you take a step you will go deeper into your subconscious mind, into your relaxed state. I'll count from ten backwards—ten down to one—and then you'll be on the bottom step, from which you'll step off into your subconscious mind."

Once I had completed that last step, we would be still. She would then ask me what I saw or what I was feeling. I would go to the part of my body that I felt was affected. At times, this would be frightening because I was unsure of this new process. Because I needed to follow through with the physical journey, she would encourage me to choose a guide to walk with me on my emotional journey.

She suggested I choose a saint, a sage or someone I trusted; I had four people I would regularly choose from. They were people who had done much good in their lives and most importantly, they were people I felt I could really trust if I had known them in real life. My guides were; Joan of Arc, Gandhi, King David (of the Old Testament) and Jesus Christ.

Because for me, these could be frightening situations, I would get comfort from their presence. They would be my silent companion or presence that reassured me when I went out on my own looking for the emotionally distressful situations that I needed to overcome. Typically, there wasn't a two-way conversation with these people. I called them into my mind to support and guide me during this process. Although, on many occasions after I forgave the person I confronted, I would ask the guide for input; that was their purpose. The guide would communicate the lesson I needed to learn from this incident. This was an enormously powerful experience! No matter the past hurt, there was *always* a lesson and positive side to it.

I would be in a situation with my uncle, grandfather or grandmother for example and didn't want to hear why things happened because I didn't believe them. Deeper down however, my spirit knew, I needed to have it revealed to me, so I could continue to grow and come to know myself. Hearing the voice of my spirit via my guide made such an impact on me and the lesson even more powerful.

The one I called upon most was Joan of Arc. I'm not sure how that happened, but I had studied her story, read a few books and watched a couple of movies about her. I was just truly inspired by the strength of her spirit and her conviction. She would be with me in her battle armor which to me, symbolized an extra layer of protection. Jesus, Gandhi and King David were just in robes, but Joan of Arc seemed to come ready to do battle on my behalf. I think I felt like we had similar spirits.

This might seem weird or far-fetched and in the beginning it was different. I knew they were creations in my mind yet, they were there for my benefit. It was deeply beneficial to take someone with me on my journey. Maybe I trusted this process because I initially learned about the idea of using 'guides' from Napoleon Hill's teachings in *Think and Grow Rich* and *Your Right to be Rich*. He talks about having guides for his life, using his mind to help him prosper and stay on top of the important areas in his life. For me, it most certainly worked!

We would come together at what we called a 'campfire'. The nature of this campfire is eternal silence, unconditional love and acceptance.

This occurred deep in my subconscious. This was a safe place for me to invite people who I wanted to talk to, who I was blaming for what happened so I could express my feelings for what they had done to me. Sometimes I would also invite people like my sisters or my parents to listen, but many times it was just between the person I needed to directly talk to and me. Even though this was in my subconscious mind, I would talk to them out loud like they were physically in front of me. The process fully encouraged me to empty out everything I was holding against that person. I would talk until I had nothing else to say.

In one session, I was mad at my grandmother for the abuse she put me through. The adult me yelled at her, cursed at her and called her names. I was furious with her. As I was yelling at her I felt that anger throughout my body. When I calmed down and asked her, "Why did you do that? Why did you hate me?"

"Well, what does your grandmother have to say to you?" asked Rachel. "Let her respond."

This is where I really opened myself up to trust in my spirit; I opened my mind to this and the words came tumbling out.

"Well, you know, I was jealous of your mom and dad," she told me harshly. "They had children and a happy marriage, your uncle never had that!"

With that, Rachel stopped me. From this place the response wasn't helping the process.

"Okay, let's go to a deeper level, Lou. What would she say from a deeper spiritual level?"

This was to help me move towards understanding and ultimately forgiveness and healing. It was here where the breakthroughs came. I allowed, me as a young child, to be present with my grandmother.

"Well, I'm very sorry. I didn't mean to cause you harm or this much pain," said my grandmother in a gentle tone as a grandmother would speak to a little boy. "You know it was not meant for us to hurt you. We were jealous of you because of how special you are. We knew you were powerful, and we were afraid of that. I'm very sorry I hurt you. I didn't know it would hurt you this much."

Rachel asked if I had a reply.

"Thank you for being honest with me," I responded and then sat for a while trying to grasp the meaning of it all. I felt like a huge burden had been lifted.

Rachel then asked if there was anything, I wanted to say to her—there was nothing. After sitting a little while longer I was able to feel the truth and allow it into me.

Now, it was time to forgive my grandmother.

"I forgive you. I forgive you with all my heart my mind and my body; I let you go. I set you free and release you."

Then it was time to forgive myself. I sat there and allowed myself to feel forgiveness like a light purifying my entire being. As part of this technique, on occasions, my guide would 'clean me out' to make sure there was no unforgiveness hiding anywhere inside. After I felt the release of those negative emotions, I became much calmer. It took some time for me to process and release her. Once I did, I let her merge into the campfire with my blessings.

Another integral part of the process was bringing my younger self into this space. This happened to me as a little boy, so it was important for the adult me to reassure him that he would never have to go through that again and from now on I would protect him. Then I would hug my younger self and let him merge inside me. Beautiful! I healed the part that received the trauma. With the merging of our parts I was becoming whole again.

When Rachel would ask what was the lesson I needed to learn, I would listen, then say what my 'guide' revealed. This was very powerful (and at first a little strange!)

At the close of one session I was told that the incident happened to me because I needed to learn to forgive and let it go. I was also to learn that I could love the person who abused me without condoning the abuse. Sometimes, the lesson was simply that I could overcome anything in my life! I could let go, forgive and move on. This growth allowed me to go out and do what I'm called to do in life.

At the start of each session, we discussed whom I wanted to forgive and one evening Rachel asked about myself.

"Would it be good to rid yourself also of the baggage from where you feel you have done things wrong or may have hurt people? Would it help to do that?"

I became so focused on the idea of forgiving others that I hadn't stopped to think I might need to forgive myself; I realized she was right. As in our previous sessions, we got into a campfire setting and I had a conversation with myself. I brought up what I felt I had done to hurt others and how I hurt myself by thinking and behaving in certain ways. The outcome was powerful. The result was the release of pent-up emotions, anger and the sense of being unforgiven.

A typical session lasted anywhere from one to two hours, depending on how much I needed to release. It would also depend on how much I listened to my inner voice and allowed the process to transpire. As I released more and more and understood how to do it, I could go deep into my subconscious mind a lot quicker. After I was calm and relaxed, I could go in and say, "Oh, yeah we need to talk about ..."

Then, at the end of each session and after whomever I was talking to had been forgiven and disappeared into the fire, I would take all the negative emotions that were left and package them up in a box. I would then wrap it with a bow, put it on the campfire and let it burn.

When that was done, I merged with my younger self. My guide and I would then scan my body and the specific body part we addressed during the session. What was and still amazes me is that all those stored negative emotions would be gone! Then that previously unhealthy-looking organ where the process started would have blood flowing through it, have a healthy color and have life again! I wonder how this has impacted my health. After we inspected the organ, and all was okay we would end the physical journey; I thanked my guide and they would leave. Then Rachel encouraged me back to full consciousness by getting me to wiggle my toes and move my fingers.

Knowing that I could overcome anything naturally started to build my confidence in other areas of my life too. Whenever my guide spoke, it was very encouraging and empowering. I was extremely grateful to know they would be alongside me on the journey. I chose them because of their purity. I chose them because of their strength. I chose them because I trusted them. I didn't need a rock star, or somebody cool to hang out with. It was more about having a teacher present. I required someone wise, spiritual and someone who I knew would see the bigger picture while they guided me. That's why I choose those four guides. I never felt uncomfortable with the idea.

Obviously, I learned to trust Rachel because of the growth and results I experienced. Just calling upon a guide, going off into my subconscious and sitting at a campfire didn't feel as crazy as it might sound. You know what it's like when you trust in someone and you believe they are there to help you. Therefore, I felt having an open mind helped me receive the most out of the therapy. I was also ready for the relief. At that point, after all the self-inquiry I was doing, I was sure something would work.

Rachel and I had built our working relationship over a number of years. When we started with the NLP, it took us a while to build mutual trust. I knew she wouldn't hurt, manipulate or guide me in any way that was detrimental. In the same way, she needed my level of commitment to be 100%! I had to really focus to get the best results. She found I was dependable and earnestly wanted healing. She was there to help me through *my* process of healing.

Remember to lookout for these things when you search for someone to help you. Look for someone with whom you can build trust and a healthy working relationship. It's like a partnership, so be wise and open to finding someone with good values who can help.

Charles and Rachel were there to ask questions, to guide and to make sure I didn't go off in the wrong direction. I trusted them, which again, is very important when looking to work with a counselor/advisor or coach to help you through the issues you face. It may take some time to build trust with your counselor, so be patient. Always remember that trust is an essential ingredient to making any support a real success. It allows you to be open to receive the healing!

19

I had many of these campfire sessions throughout 2010 and 2011, leading up to the one where I finally confronted the woman who had sex with my uncle in front of me. Up until that time, I had no idea of the huge importance of that event. I think most people who heard about what happened would not see the woman as being a big problem. They would have thought my uncle's actions were a bigger issue, but that's not how my mind dealt with it.

I'll explain what happened in the hopes that it will help you understand the significant role it played in my life, so you can learn too. That session was very telling. I still remember a great deal of it, one of those 'like it happened yesterday' things because it was so impactful for my future.

Leading up to that point, I was considering the idea of being married again. The divorce was final in 2008 and as I started dating, I realized I was changing and growing. When I met someone, who had too many issues, which could cause an unhealthy relationship, I could tell. My heart would feel it. On a date, I would feel that something was not right; I didn't know exactly what it was, but I could just sense a problem.

Even if there was some 'chemistry', I could hear that inner voice trying to tell me a relationship wouldn't work. Sometimes I ignored it and got into a relationship with someone because I just wanted to have one—I knew it wasn't right. There were times I was impatient and tried to force it. As I let go of my past, I became more and more aware of what I wanted and what would or would not work for me. I also became more independent and self-reliant, so I grew not to 'need' someone.

As I healed and progressed, I started to realize that I now liked different traits in a person and was no longer attracted to the same type of person as before. I had always been attracted to someone who was beautiful, in good health and productive, but there was more to it. There had to be more depth to them. I realized that there were a lot of wounded people who would bring their problems into their relationships. This was not for me.

We *all* have issues and struggles in life, yet this was about finding someone who was also on a forward path of awareness and learning to work through their issues. One thing I did that helped me clarify what I desired was to sit in a quiet place and make a list of what I was looking for in a spouse. I wrote down the qualities of what I wanted in a woman, with all the principles of success and setting goals and writing them down I thought why not? So, I did. I set myself very high standards and I wrote down over 50 qualities. Here is an actual copy of the list dated 08/21/07.

8/21/07

SOMEWHERE IN ANOTHER JOURNAL I
THOUGHT I WROTE A DESCRIPTION OF
MY NEXT & HOPEFULLY FINAL WIFE.
BUT I HAVE NOT LOCATED THAT DESCRIPTION
& TODAY LISTENING TO BRIAN TRACY IT
TRIGGERED ME TO WRITE OUT MANY
QUALITIES ON A STICKY NOTE SO I
AM CAPTURING THEM HERE BECAUSE I
BELIEVE...

QUALITIES / VALUES / CHARACTERISTICS OF MY PARTNER

1 GREAT COMMUNICATOR
2 CONFIDENT
3 CALM
4 HONEST
5 Athletic
6 Has a Vision & Purpose Aligned w/or mine   *Have a common purpose w/ me!*   → *compliments mine*
7 Supportive
8 Beautiful
9 LOVING
10 INTEGRITY
11 Christian
12 Personal Growth oriented & Dedicated
    TO LIFE LONG SELF Improvement / Development.
13 Involved / Active & Supportive in Mommy & CEE
14 Allows the Man to Lead w/o a Power Struggle
15 Independent
16 LOVES OUTDOORS

147

8/9/07 QUALITIES CONTINUED

17 Active/worker
18 Serving Heart
19 Loves children / Good with children
20 Patient
21 Goal oriented
22 Spiritually Attuned / In Tune
23 Positive / Optimistic
24 Trustworthy
25 Trusting
26 Sweet
27 Respectful
28 Passionate
29 Observant
30 Interactive
31 Enjoys Physical Activity
32 Enjoys Travel
33 Intelligent
34 Patient
35 Giving
36 Diligent
37 Self-controlled
38 Merciful
39 Loyal
40 Fun
41 Flexible
42 Stable
43 Productive
44 Willing to Learn

8/7/07

45 Romantic
46 Willing to Follow
47 LEADER
48 DREAMER
49 Completor/Complimentor
50 COMPETENT
51 Healthy - MIND - BODY - SPIRIT
52 CONSIDERATE

My thinking was: Why settle for less than I wanted or even deserved? I was working so hard on myself to become the man worthy of the woman I described in my journal, so why shouldn't I have a wife with all those qualities? Hopefully, my list would make finding a 'match' easier, but possibly more time-consuming. I relied on my Faith, meeting people, and knowing what I wanted in a spouse.

When I had that very significant session around mid-October 2011, I was single, investing time with my son and business, but knew I really needed to invest more time on my healing. I contacted Rachel and set an appointment. At this point, we were working via phone and Skype because her husband's job moved them out of state.

I recall our process of relaxing and discussing the starting point and then we got into a campfire journey. As I opened-up, I invited my uncle and an unknown woman to join me in the scene. Since I was so very young when this incident occurred, I was yet to learn who this woman was as I allowed her to be present.

At first, I was talking to my uncle as an adult, protecting the younger me. I was yelling and cursing at him because I was so mad that he had sex with this woman in front of me, laughing at me while he had his way with her. Then I turned to the woman.

"How could you do that to a child?!" "How could you? You're a mother of three children. How could a mother do that in front of a child?" Not knowing this woman, I was a bit surprised when I heard the words come out my mouth. The point was; in addition to still being so mad at her I knew she had children? How did that work?

"That was disgusting! Shame on you for doing that to me!" I yelled. "I was just a child and you were ruining my life."

At first, she simply replied, "You know, I was having fun with your uncle." I started to get angrier, but Rachel intervened and asked: "How would she respond on a deeper level?"

Then we went deeper into the spirit, and I said, "You know that was wrong." I said, "How could you do that? I don't understand. I'm so mad at you."

I don't know what I called her, but there were many names. I was so mad that this woman would stoop to a level to have sex in front of a child; she was a woman and should have shown more concern for someone so young. Again, this was all occurring in my subconscious mind, but somewhere in my spirit, I was seeing her older now, as a mother, yet 40 years ago, she wasn't a mom. Then she replied to me.

"Well, you're right. I am very sorry. I am so happy that you brought me here to resolve this. This has been with me all my life, I am so very sorry. I have three children of my own now and I have protected them, so this would never happen to them. Would you please forgive me? I have carried this with me all my life."

Now I was deeply sobbing. Not understanding all of this but allowing the process to continue. We talked it out a little more, then I said, "Thank you for being honest with me, and thank you for asking to be forgiven." Then Rachel asked if there was anything else that needed to be said, but there wasn't.

Then I said, "I forgive you with all my heart and soul, from the top of my head to the bottom of my heart, with all my body, all my being. I forgive you and I release you and let you go."

When I did that, I felt the release like a flood washing through me. It was here I realized that deep down, no matter how nicely I treated women—and I was always respectful and caring— there was something inside me that put up barriers. I had a deep-seated anger towards what happened with this woman and could never have a truly healthy relationship with anyone until I forgave her. Imagine this? How would anyone, including me have known this until I started on this journey of self-inquiry? Amazing!

After I forgave this woman, I became grateful for her too. Yes, it's true. I learned to be *grateful* for this woman. Even though I had dragged that old scene around with me way deep down in my mind for all those years, I count it as a blessing that I was able to forgive her and be grateful to learn to forgive. Within a couple of months of letting go of the incident with this woman, I met the love of my life! Was it all a coincidence?

As hurtful as these incidents were, I am grateful for the lessons I learned from these people. It may seem very strange, even with all the abuse that I suffered at the hands of my uncle, he is probably one the biggest gifts in my life! Because of this, it drove me to want to be free.

Free of those misunderstood emotions and issues in my life. Free of all the sensitivity, worthlessness and the self-hatred. Without those horrible incidents, I probably would have never gone through these processes of learning and growing. I may have not had the same level of hurt but everyone has some type of unforgiveness which manifests itself into other areas that we all tend to accept and live with. Instead, I would be sulking, just being a mediocre guy never getting out of myself. I would be self-medicating surviving, and doing the least to get by in life, never really growing to become a different person. The person I wanted and now felt I deserved to be.

20

I have another uncle who, after my father died became like a second dad to me. He was always on my side, encouraging me to make sure I treated myself well and enjoyed my life. One day, while still in the process of my divorce and in need of new thinking, I was complaining to him about my situation.

"Louie, let me tell you something," he said. "I am a Catholic and I may not be a very good one, ***BUT*** I don't think Christ died so you could live a miserable life! Learn to be happy!"

That statement was so powerful for me! I read the Bible and prayed every day, but somehow, I missed that completely. Now, as I turned the key to my office door years later, I knew how right he had been. Once I started to apply faith in my life, after I forgave those who hurt me, as I prepared myself to be a man of value and as I let go of my negative beliefs, I met Leslie. God had listened to my prayers and recognized my conviction then blessed me with my beautiful wife.

Those same beliefs in myself, trusting and believing that good things were going to happen in my life, as well as my personal growth, also greatly impacted my business. I think back to those early years, when cash flow was very limited, and I remember one time when I was waiting on a very large payment from a client. It was already past due, yet the client was slow in processing and thought it may be another two or more weeks before I received the payment. I needed it to make payroll and some very necessary payments to our suppliers, who were getting tired of waiting for their money.

During that time, I had a session with Rachel. What came out was that, deep down, I was holding onto something so tight that

I wouldn't let go... A belief that I was closed off to was what she called receiving good in my life. Once I worked through that old belief I let it go. Incredibly, within the next three days this six-figure check showed up in the mail, saving me from financial embarrassment.

Now, I know it wasn't a total miracle; the money was owed to me, was overdue and I needed it by a certain day. However, from my clients' feedback, it would still be weeks before they sent it. I was sure I was going to get it late, jeopardizing my business. Once I let go of that false belief and increased my faith, there was the check on my desk. It was another confirmation to let go and believe. I started to understand though my experience that our inner thoughts and beliefs have a huge impact on our lives good or bad, right or wrong, healthy or unhealthy. This is true for all of us.

As we got into the deeper levels with the journey sessions, my beliefs changed and began to take hold. I started to act differently and draw different conclusions about things in my life; I was good, I deserved to be happy and that good things would happen to me. Once I believed and expected those things, I started to live a much better life!

When I started my business, it was me, a computer and a tool bag working out of a converted screened-in room at the back of my house. After almost a year, I moved into an office located in our local downtown where many old homes were converted into office and commercial spaces. This old home was far from newly remodeled, but it worked for my first base of operations. On the first floor was a bridal salon, the second and third floors each comprised several small 10' x 12' office rooms off a central hallway.

For the first year it was fine, then I expanded from two offices to three. As I grew there, I realized the building was a mess, but it took someone walking in the door to really make me see the truth.

"Hey!" said a woman in her forties as she poked her head around the door one morning.

"Hi, can I help you?"

"Yeah, I'm looking for some office space. I saw this place has some space for rent, for my husband, for his company."

"What does he do?" I asked as she stepped further into the room.

"Oh, he's in construction and he needs an office."

"Oh, okay. It's not great here, but it's alright."

She started to look around more, and I saw her brow furrow.

"Really? This place looks like a dump to me!" As she investigated the unkempt ragged empty offices...

I looked around and, quite suddenly, I saw what she meant.

"Yeah, good point!" I said sheepishly as she shook her head and walked out, waving a hand in thanks over her shoulder.

I hired an assistant just prior to that and realizing I needed nicer surroundings, we moved the office. One very important aspect of my business was as I grew, the company grew, many changes were happening in parallel. As I worked on opening my mind to receive good things, I realized I could expand. As I cleared space in my head by releasing those old negative emotions and limiting beliefs, I had room to solve more problems, to be creative and allow my life to expand too. I would tell myself I was becoming healthier, and wealthier in my thinking. It allowed me to become 'healthier' in all my business dealings. So that day we started looking for somewhere much newer and nicer.

A month or so later, we moved into a new office. It was beautiful! The previous occupant was a judge who had brought in an interior designer! As I settled into this new space, I realized I didn't have to endure a hard life and I certainly didn't need to be surrounded by garbage and junk. I deserved to be somewhere nice! I was living like life was something to be endured rather than to be enjoyed. I finally started to believe I should—and now *would*—take care of myself.

I put myself in a healthy environment, a warm and welcoming environment ... that was such a total shift for me! This was happening as I was moving out of the marital home and not long after we found the new office. Guess where I found a new, quiet place to live? Oh, only about 10 houses down a side street from my new office. The location was great, I could walk to my office and later when my son was accepted to his High School, we could easily walk to the train, so he could get to school without a hassle. The events in my life seemed to be lining up. Hmmm, were these all coincidences, a reflection of my growth or God's grace smiling upon me? Perhaps all of them. I believe they were happening *because* of my growth.

For years, I felt worthless, especially after being in a marriage where I was constantly put down and then going through the divorce. Now, I was moving to a place where I would have peace and build myself up which was about the same time, I was ready to progress into some forgiveness.

In one of those sessions with Rachel, I had realized that I had issues with my parents, even though they had no idea of what happened. Had they known about the cruelty and abuse, they would have never left us in their care.

Unfortunately, during this session, I was dealing with an overwhelming amount of baggage from my past. I felt a lot of anger towards them for not protecting me.

I remember standing there as a little boy, crying during another session. "Why didn't you pay more attention to us?" I was having a hard time wrapping my head around how they couldn't know what was happening with my uncle. "All those times you were out, weren't you worried about us? You didn't even question anything that happened when we were alone with him! Why didn't you ask me what happened the night, he threw me down the stairs and into the basement?"

There was so much energy in that session, a lot of anger and some very strong feelings. For so many years I had done a very good job of suppressing all those emotions. Now after releasing my anger and hurt, I could let all those thoughts go and clear out my mind.

In this intensely powerful and spiritual setting, I was talking to my parents as if they were physically present. As with all the campfire sessions, I was talking out loud, to be heard as I released my bottled-up feelings. Working within the nature of eternal silence and unconditional love, I was telling them exactly how I felt as a boy, when those terrible things occurred. Now, I felt free to tell them all the thoughts I had wanted to tell them as a child but couldn't.

By this time, my dad had been gone for many years, I couldn't truly tell him anything. My sessions with Rachel allowed me to have those deep and very necessary conversations with my dad and mom. Working through it, I was able to forgive them. Sitting there and feeling the release of all the anger and bitterness while allowing the forgiveness deep within my heart, was just truly incredible. I wish I could accurately express, to you just how good it felt.

21

After the session with my parents I noticed that my relationship with my mom improved. There was nothing specific, but I could see and feel that it was easier. It wasn't as strained as it had once been, I was much more relaxed when interacting with her. This change enabled me to act in a more loving way, which considering this stage in our lives allowed us to have the mother, son relationship we both genuinely needed.

At one point before the divorce, I had an argument with my mom. There were little things that happened, but my ex-wife blew them out of proportion and frankly forced me to say something, so I felt like I had to stick up for her.

"If you are going to continue to treat us like this, you won't see us anymore," I told my mom, and her face just dropped. There really weren't any issues, and I didn't need to threaten her. This had come from my ex-wife, but at that time, I couldn't see it. I wasn't mentally strong enough to see the misconceptions or to stand up for myself or use more love and understanding with my mom. After the session where I let go and learned my new beliefs, our relationship changed and continues to be healthy and growing. Today my mom and I have a wonderful relationship. We talk and visit often. She even worked to help me with some parts of my business.

Another very beneficial session I had along the way was when I let go of the pain from not getting to say goodbye to my dad before he died. In the session with my dad I was able to sit and talk to him, give him a hug and say goodbye. It settled my spirit immensely. I became calmer and used the experience to help build a better relationship with my son; just by having that closure with my dad, I could now have a better relationship with my son. As I drove home one evening, I thought, "Wow! I couldn't make this stuff up!"

My son and I were now able to sensibly talk through life issues. If he did something that I didn't want him to do, I didn't yell at him. Instead, I explained why I didn't want him doing whatever it was. Through this stable approach we developed a deeper, calmer relationship. I made a conscious decision not to hold on to hurt and anger as I had years before. He could sense the change and became more forgiving. We continued to have meaningful conversations and interactions. This healing work opened me up to be able to have better relationships all around. Forgiveness is such a powerful force.

I needed to forgive my uncle. After a very intense session, we found I was still holding onto a great deal of anger towards him. I felt my chest constricting and was breathing so heavily it felt as if I had just run up five flights of stairs. I yelled at him repeatedly. The emotion was so powerful, as it came from the depths of my soul. It felt like I was breathing fire from my lungs. The energy that I was suppressing was extremely negative. A few days after I released those emotions, I ended up with a chest cold. My lungs were inflamed from the heavy, negative energy. As I released the bitter anger towards my aggressors, I became much healthier.

I grew in wisdom, discernment and awareness through my daily reading of Proverbs. I developed better people skills and could see, in others, just like me, they had their own issues. I may not know where their issues came from, but I knew that they were dealing with something. Everyone handles their 'stuff' in different ways. I've learned to extend grace to others because you never really know what's going on behind the scenes.

Being more aware allowed me to notice what was going on in my surroundings; it helped me in many ways. One way was learning to be empathetic, and another was that I could sense which people to avoid. For example, while looking for a new bride, when I went on a date, I would see how sensitive or angry or defensive she was, which was an indication to me that she had something unresolved going on inside her. I also learned to listen to her words and watch her actions. Were they positive or negative?

There was a girl I dated at one time, whom I suspected had been abused. She confided in me that she had been abused and it was a pattern in her life. I tried to get her help. She went for one session with Rachel but wouldn't see it through, and our relationship ended.

This newfound perceptiveness kept me aware of what was going on in my own life. It allowed me to be open and to question things like situations at work, with customers and employees. Because I was letting go of the negative, I could sense what was happening which opened me to see it. I was awakening my mind to better see what was going on around me. Because my mind was no longer pushing negative feelings down into my body, I was able to be more alert and broader in my thinking.

I continued letting those emotions out and processing them like we all should. When you sense a negative feeling and the emotion goes through you like a wave, you get to respond. You don't have to hold on to it and you don't have to suppress it. You don't have to lash out in anger; instead, just let the wave go through you then let it go. When I finally experienced my emotions, I felt whole as a human being. This was an enormous factor in allowing myself to grow and become healthier.

At times, the journey would take me directly to someone I needed to confront from my past. Other times I would go to a part of my body that I sensed was ailing. Sometimes it would be my liver or my stomach or another internal organ. For me this meant that I was holding on to a negative emotion in that specific part of my body causing it to fail. It was now time to release that toxic emotion. That meant meeting the person who I identified with as the cause of that emotional distress. I remember specifically one time I was struggling. I was tired and sluggish. It seemed like something was going on inside my body. We had another session where we did a physical journey. Again, through my subconscious, I went deep into my body and discovered that part my liver was black and had a foul smell. It looked like it was dying. I found that the suppressed anger, hatred, and bitterness towards my uncle was being stored there. After that session when I cleared those negative emotions and forgave my uncle, my liver started healing. An interesting incident occurred; I had a pre-scheduled blood test the following day. When we received the results, we found my liver enzymes were very high. My doctor was astonished and wanted to know if I'd been drinking alcohol the night prior to my test. I hadn't. My liver was sick because of my suppressing those toxic emotions attached to my previous concerns. The release of negative emotions seemed to spike the test; quite soon after that, my liver was confirmed to be working perfectly.

There have been so many connections to my health with these processes. As I released the anger and stopped holding issues; in my gut, in my heart, my lungs, my stomach and my brain and my body started 'working better'. I was able to perform better in the gym, be more effective and less tired at work, and stay healthy and happy.

22

Detaching from the unhealthy relationships in my life also helped me in business. I had some 'unhealthy' customers who wouldn't pay me on time or sought to make me renegotiate terms *after* we had made an agreement and had a signed contract.

I remember one time sitting in front of a man who ran a small generic pharmaceutical manufacturing company. He needed service work, which after a significant discount totaled $11,000.00. After the work was satisfactorily completed and invoiced, he delayed payment. He asked me to come to his office to collect the check. I asked him to send it in the mail, he refused to pay. When I got there he wanted to negotiate the price. We went back and forth for two hours to get us to $9,000.00. So, it cost me two hours of my time and $2,000.00 of my money to get a portion of what he legitimately owed me. This was how *he* did business. It was also how I had allowed him to treat me in business then too ... but not anymore.

For him, it was important to renegotiate after he agreed to the original terms; that was his company's culture. He took advantage of our agreement! I thought well, this is not how I do business. This is America! I am an American citizen and my word is my bond! It's okay to have different cultures here, the USA was founded on values and diversity, but ethics and integrity transcend culture. This became about me learning to become stronger and more confident. I am always happy to negotiate, but once the deal is agreed upon, there is no more game playing. Things can and do change, so when needed we would discuss and come to full agreement with all parties. This wasn't about that. It was about me learning to set boundaries, say no and stand up for myself!

Because I had already performed additional work, I had one more situation like that with the same guy. He said he was not going to pay the full amount, so I simply told him I would take him to court.

"You won't take me to court for this amount," he said flippantly, "because if you do, it would cost you more than this. Just take my offer and you'll get paid."

Now I put up a boundary, I put up a wall, and before I put the phone down, I said:

"This is business. You agreed to it; I agreed to it. I will see you in court, so let's go."

He finally paid me $3,000 of the $4,000 he owed, but the next time he called to get some work done, I simply told him to go somewhere else. I was finally standing up for myself! Compared to before when I didn't have the strength to do that. I would simply accept it because of that old belief system and would once more be beaten down.

This 'new me' came from an amazing journey and process of discovery. Self-development or self-inquiry might be other ways to describe it, but it was about realizing; " I'm not who those people said I was and I'm not the old person I thought I was. I decided I was no longer going to be treated with disrespect. Nor was I going to be a receptacle for their garbage or a recipient of their abuse." I am created in the image of God. I needed to learn how that manifested in my life.

As I let go of what happened all those years ago, sought God's peace and took responsibility for my actions, I became healthier, stronger. As I forgave and let go of all that baggage, I had more self-awareness and a growing confidence. Now, I could stand up and professionally say, "No, call someone else, good luck."

OR "If you would like then we can go to court. Is that what you would like?"

A short while after I let go of my relationship with that bad payer, there was another long-term client who owed me $7,500.00. I knew they were having some financial issues. They were always slow payers, but I befriended one of the managers and always liked to help them out. Then the owner of the company called.

"I will pay you $5,000.00 if you come today and help us fix more equipment," she said, naming some more problems.

"The cost of doing that will be more than $5,000.00. If you agree to pay me the $7,500 you already owe, I will come today."

"No, I will pay you $5,000 and give you the rest later."

"If that's the case, then I'm not coming out."

"But I won't pay you anything if you don't come."

"That's fine; we will go to court."

With that case we did, but I knew I wasn't going to get the money afterwards. It has been in court for many years because they went bankrupt; a multimillion-dollar corporation that went out of business. But I stood up for myself because I realized I was going to incur another $5,000 on top of what they already owed and no guarantee of getting paid for that. I could be doing something better with my time; I could find new clients who would pay me and create real income. I could grow my company and help my employees instead of going out there and acting like a slave to these types of people.

The whole transition process is ongoing, and recently I had an issue with the CEO of the new company and sent him a letter via FedEx. He replied a week later in an email with some very unprofessional things. Five or six years ago, I would have thought he was right, and I would have listened to him.

Instead, I was angry with the guy. I thought he was immature and unprofessional. I wondered how he got to be a CEO of a company with over 600 employees. I was really looking forward to getting out of there.

He thought he was in a position of power and sought to use that over who I was for the company's benefit. He was a CEO, but so was I, and I told him so in no uncertain terms. No matter who we are in life, we deserve to be treated as free people, not slaves or indentured servants or under someone's control for manipulative reasons. Because he was in a titled and senior position doesn't mean he should have power over who I was and who I was becoming. Unfortunately, in today's world, there are many employees who allow their situations to become unhealthy, codependent, even debilitating. Deep down I knew I was born free and would be able to create my own future. Finally, through all my work, I accepted that fact!

My company was still growing, and I had somebody who was interested in buying it. However, he offered me only about 25% of what I wanted. When I took a step back, I realized that there was still work to be done to grow the business and I needed to finish what I started.

I turned down that first and second offers for the company because the value was too low. I continued to grow my business and achieved my goal. I sold the business for what I wanted and what it was worth. I have married the wife I desired, based on a healthy view and those 52 qualities. She has more than met those! I wanted a loving and growing relationship with my son. We have it! God knew what I needed, so He gave me a bonus with all of it!

It took me a long time to hit these goals—five years for one, and eight for the others—but I had to let go of all that emotional junk and become the person who could trust others. I had to persevere and work. I had to become the man who would treat a woman in the manner God would have me treat her. It is not a magic trick or a quick fix. I had to be ready for the best partner, and for me, that took some time. Yes, I asked God for help during that earnest prayer in my kitchen and, as usual, He came through. He knew I was sincere and ready to receive.

Along with that, I also believe in that creative power of our minds. I had to know what I wanted while becoming the man who was worthy of this woman. This was where my part was; I had to put in the time to develop, to grow and clearly define my goals. Again, I did my homework. This was a focused effort over many long lonely years, but boy has it all been worth it!

God is a creator. He is *THE Creator*. If He made us in His image, then aren't we little creators too? You know, we must ask the question, "What do I want in my future?" This is part of the reason I had to write this book so I can help people grow and create the life they want. I had to go through the pains of deep releasing and forgiving, **lots** of change and growth, but I wouldn't go back and change anything that happened. Now, I can see that there was a reason for everything I went through.

Selling my company was extremely stressful but has also been worth it. Now I am free to go do what I really want to do which is to help others build their own businesses, to speak, to write and embolden people so they can be set free like I was.

Long ago, I created the picture of what I wanted my life to be. In my mind and heart, I visualized a beautiful new wife, a great relationship with my son, a successful business that I have since sold, and a new life! I am not tied down anymore to that past life. I believe in the creation theory and that everything can work for the good of those who believe. When we know what we want and work hard for it, we can succeed. 'It' may look a little different when we achieve our goals, and success doesn't always come right when we want it but remaining steadfast to our visions will help it to occur.

If things seem late or don't go according to plan, then remember, I'll say it again, that everything happens for a reason. There is always a bigger plan. We don't always know the 'why' until much later, but that's another huge lesson for all of us. Believing in Providence is important, believing that things happen for a reason is important, but we can't sit around and wait for things to happen; we all need to give our dreams a nudge, get to work, give things some help, some encouragement, some guidance, and so on. We must *work* for our dreams! They just don't fall into our lap. When it comes to making your dreams a reality there is no lottery!

If you have any issues or baggage in your life, letting go of and forgiving whomever or whatever caused those problems is going to equip you for creating the life or destiny that you want. You need to accept that you really can do something to create your own future. Just like I did. In fact, you **must** be an active participant in your future, or you will simply get whatever life deals you. It is your choice.

In 2012, while my son was still in high school, I got a chance to visit High Point University, in High Point, North Carolina. This may sound crazy but as soon as I stepped off the bus, I knew I wanted him to go there. As I walked the promenade, I 'got it'! I saw that the entire campus was intentionally and deliberately designed to create an environment of success. There was a feeling or sense of excellence while walking around. It was like someone took the time to create a place where students could learn, grow, and become the best person they could become. It was like no other place I have visited! A university of success! High Point is becoming the premier life skills university in our country, in an era when life skills are greatly needed. I recommend you check out their campus and website. www.highpoint.edu - Even if you don't have someone going to college it would be worth your time and energy to investigate what's going on there.

It reminded me, in a much bigger way of course, of what I was creating in my home during all those years of studying, growth, and healing. I came home so excited to discuss it with my son, but I had to plant seeds to see if he would decide to attend. With some guidance from the University's President and me, he committed to the school and then it all fell into place.

My initial reason for even being in High Point was to attend a business seminar, which had nothing to do with the University. This event turned out to be an overpriced sale-a-thon to get us to buy more seminars and coaching. I didn't care however, because something great came out of it. I can now see, that just like all the adversity I faced in my life; a lot of good came out of it. The price I paid was more than worth it! We must learn to find that "silver lining" in everything we experience. No complaining or criticizing. Learn to be optimistic!

Another blessing from that visit was meeting the University's President, Dr. Nido Qubein - www.nidoqubein.com

As a benefit of that relationship, Nido has mentored me and introduced me to some of his associates. One of those relationships is with Jim Stovall. I met Jim outside High Point University a few years before but had the opportunity to meet in person while he was on campus. We have since grown to become friends and associates. There is no way that a guy with a tech school diploma, some entry level corporate experience and years of law enforcement experience should have accomplished some of these things and befriended some of these people!

I now feel more than just alive. My son is smart, on track and terrific! My wife is beautiful, intelligent and successful! Being a person with no training, I built, grew, and sold a successful and sustainable company. I am on my way up when most people who are in their 50's are becoming stagnate or are on their way down. I am still moving in the right direction, and with the right frame of mind. Why can't that happen for you? I know it can!

I will be eternally grateful Charles, Rachel, Brad, and my many other advisors. They have given of themselves. Their kindness and caring and their expertise have helped me prosper where otherwise I would have been lost. Again, I realize how important my quiet time was and still is. It is the time that I invested in *myself.* I learned to do what I needed to do to nourish my soul. As much as we want to care for others, we must care for ourselves. There is nothing wrong with personal or 'selfish time'.

You must also accept, as I most certainly have, that none of this would be possible without the grace of God. My prayer time, the prayers of others who cared, my study and application of the Bible were and are paramount to this entire process. Please know that, with all the therapeutic methods I've tried and experienced, there were some (not mentioned) that didn't work or fit with my beliefs. With those I did pursue, I went into them with an open mind and the belief that God was guiding me through the process.

I prayed for help, and when it appeared, I went for it. Yes, I had to use discernment, but I also had to be open to some very different ideas that I thought were well, weird and maybe even a little far-fetched. With my roots in Christianity, I felt confident that I would only benefit from these processes. I give The Good Lord credit for being my best friend, savior, mentor, guide, and my source of power and energy.

An important realization was; I was also grieving each time I went through the forgiveness process. Although based in fear, I was letting go of something that was previously important to me. In some way, I missed it when it was gone. For all of us it is very important to allow the grieving process to occur. To help me get over these incidents and progress through a healing process, I spent time in nature, time with friends, watched inspiring movies, listened to music or played my guitar. I listened to a lot of different kinds of music but seemed to gravitate to uplifting music, where the artists were talking about going through or overcoming their own struggles.

I grew up playing the guitar and listening to music, which came naturally. As I matured and discovered self-development while building my own company, I mainly listened to business and motivational audios, things to keep me growing. I found I started to dry up without music. Adding music back into my life was a welcome friend and greatly helped me through many tough times. Today, I still work to keep my listening balanced with business and inspirational materials and inspiring music. A little bit of each every day is a good mix for me.

As I was establishing these habits, they became part of my daily routine. The time I first met with Rachel, I was also trying to be nicer to myself. I had to understand and accept that a lot of the hatred I felt towards others I pointed at *me*. More importantly I did this because I never wanted to hurt anyone else. I shoved the buildup of negative emotions from all those abusive events it deep down inside! That's why I buried all the negative experiences … to keep it away from others.

That wasn't a good approach! I'm sure during the years of turmoil and healing, I have hurt others. For that, I apologize and ask for forgiveness.

During those years, I tried desperately to internalize everything. I didn't want anyone to see how fearful and angry I was. There was so much bitterness and hatred. Because of shame and guilt, I continually directed it towards myself.

With all that junk going on inside, I really didn't trust people, which made me try to control everything to make it all perfect. It had to be. Perfect was a keyword for me. Not excellent, but *perfect*. Later, I learned how to apply these words in my life because they were not interchangeable. Rachel helped me see that having time to myself to do what I liked to do was vital to breaking those issues. I could do whatever I wanted to; I could listen to whatever I wanted to and choosing something different was good. I could like some music a bit or a lot, but what I listened to did not have to be perfect. In other words, before I didn't trust that my life was a journey with a meandering path, but more like some straight line from A to B, from birth to death that could not be deviated from.

A lot of my healing time was spent learning to recognize my feelings, to trust myself, to trust God, to trust His Universe, so I had to be open to it. The sessions with Rachel helped me and the music helped me relax when I was on my own. I stopped trying to 'conquer the world' albeit it was a very small world. I spent time contemplating things as well, just trying to work out where I was going, to occasionally shift into neutral to slow down and to pay attention to my life.

I intentionally grew more meditative and learned critical thinking skills. I have always been a doer, someone who is action oriented. I was very conscious of trying to shift that, to become a more of a thinker. When the pendulum swung very much in that direction, it got stuck there for a while and it almost paralyzed me because of over-analysis! What I was learning is that there is room for both in my life and it was very crucial for a healthy significant life to learn to balance those very important parts of me.

I had a friend ask, "What are you running from in such a hurry?" I replied, "I'm in a hurry to get away from my old life!" I got into a rut of always trying to fix myself, which for a while, as I mentioned earlier, caused an addictive approach to self-improvement. This seems to be common with people in our society. We attend a seminar or listen to a recording and feel better for a few days or weeks, but then the feeling goes away. Then we need our fix again, and the cycle repeats itself. I had to let go of the idea that there was something *wrong* with me, when, after all this work there really wasn't. There never was anything *wrong* with me except for my thinking.

My daily routine was a way for me to disrupt my old unhealthy patterns of thinking and living. The quiet time was a disrupter to that and helped me soften and listen to God more and to my deeper self. This way, I could sense those bad feelings and let them go, instead of suppressing them and shoving them down inside me. I also realized it was better to address these hurtful situations immediately or within a reasonable amount of time instead of just ignoring them. Which freed me up to handle more important issues in my life.

I realized that I could choose which voice to listen to and how to respond. Listening to someone else who reinforced the new behaviors, whether it was a preacher, businessman, Amway audios, Napoleon Hill, Nido Qubein, or other speakers helped me start to think differently.

To help me continue to learn the new habit, I used note cards and captured a thought I liked or one I wanted to make part of my life that showed I was healthy, or I was good at a skill, etc. After writing it down I would repeat it in the form of positive self-talk. I probably have several hundred cards with different sayings and quotes. Now I use different cards for skills and goal-based habits.

As well as the emotional, spiritual, and mental processes, there was, of course, the physical side. Again, I was working out five to six days a week, for about an hour a day and it would be high intensity interval training with a mix of resistance or weights or some athletic training. I started to get my body healthy and balanced. Wendy my trainer, taught me better ways to challenge my body. She helped educate me on using my whole body through balance, stabilization and functional exercises. I was developing my whole person, my mind, spirit, emotions, will and physical structure.

It sounds silly, but I even trained myself how to talk and use more agreeable facial expressions, inflections, cadence, and so on. Many years prior to meeting Charles and Rachel, I didn't smile a lot of course, now I know why. Once I was aware of this and able to do something about it, I read and re-read *How to Win Friends and Influence People* by Dale Carnegie. In one chapter, he talks about smiling, so I looked in the mirror and relearned how to smile. I had to have a genuine smile so it didn't look like I was smirking. All these things should have been natural to me as a human, but because I was so hurt and angry, I had to retrain myself to become a healthy person.

All these day-to-day habits added up. I was very diligent about it for many years until they became a part of me. Today, if I go more than a day without reading or praying or exercising, or feeling my emotions, I think something is missing.

PART 4

NEW BEGINNINGS

"We must be willing to get rid of the life we have planned, so as to have the life that is waiting for us. The old skin has to be shed before the new one can come."

—Joseph Campbell

23

In early December 2011, a friend's girlfriend had cajoled me into going on yet another blind date for dinner. I didn't want to go at first but then changed my mind and found that, despite us not really being suited for one another, we had a fun evening. After that mid-October session with Rachel, where I let go of my anger towards that unknown woman, I found myself much more relaxed about the idea of a serious relationship. Over the holidays, I even found myself wishing I could have been with someone, someone who would become more important to me.

On January the 2nd 2012, I was standing in my kitchen and thinking about the release of all the hatred and anger mixed with the unhealthy experiences of dating over the past years. With all of that running through my mind, I felt I was finally ready to move and have someone in my life. I was ready for a *real* relationship and felt the desire to meet the right person, make it work and be happy. It was a strange feeling because I knew I was deeply changing. Once more, I was letting go of my old beliefs, which related to how I reacted to people and how I treated myself in a relationship. So, I opened my heart and my mind to God.

"Okay, Lord, you've got me. I'm ready. I don't want this junk anymore. I don't want any unhealthy relationships. I want the right woman in my life."

Nothing noticeable happened for all of *two weeks*... Then I met Leslie!

At that time, I attended Liquid Church which was in a Hyatt Hotel where they held non-denominational Sunday Christian services in the ballroom. They have now grown enough to build their own place. When the service was over, I went out to the mezzanine level heading to the men's room, and there she was. My whole vision was filled with the image of this incredibly beautiful woman. She was dressed in a thigh-length mink coat, jeans and hiking boots and I thought, oh, my gosh! Who *is* that woman? Then I felt this incredibly deep stirring in my chest. It's no exaggeration to say that she completely took my breath away.

I immediately walked right past her because I was running to the restroom and failed to catch her eye. So, feeling like a love-struck teenager, I got out of there as quickly as I could while saying a prayer: "God, please let her still be there when I get back." She was there and this time she smiled at me. I immediately walked up to her and started a conversation. She told me she was there with some friends who were inside registering to volunteer.

"This is your first time here then?" I asked, and she nodded her head.

"So, did you like the service?"

"Well kind of ..." she replied noncommittally.

"So, you didn't like it?" I suggested.

"Well not really ..." she replied, looking a little sheepish and no doubt thinking I was a huge devotee.

"Well, you know, I always heard you should try a church three times," I replied with a smile, "you never know what you get and it could be for you."

"Yeah, I guess so," she said, looking a little more relaxed.

"I've been here for years. I tried it several times and decided to stick with it and now I love it."

"Well, I suppose I could try it one more time!" It was her turn to smile.

We talked a little bit more about what she did for a living and what I did, I asked her if she had a card and she shook her head.

"Well, here is my card," I said pulling one out of my wallet, "if I can answer any questions, please call me."

She thanked me and I managed to drag myself away and walked down a level to the restaurant and bar area where I ordered some dinner and a glass of wine. When I took my first sip, my hands were shaking but for good reasons this time.

It was football season, so I was trying to distract myself from thinking about her by watching the playoffs. About ten minutes later, I was interrupted by someone; it was Helen, the woman I had dinner with on that blind date. We didn't connect as a potential couple but had become friends.

"Hey, Lou, I've been texting you all day; did you get my messages?"

"Well, no, but I recently changed my number and I don't think I've seen you since."

"Oh, no worries; I'll grab it from you sometime, but what I was trying to tell you was that I brought a friend of mine with me today and want you to meet her."

"Well, I'm eating right now, can I come by later?"

"Oh sure, no problem. We can get something too, then I'll come find you again."

Helen turned up again thirty minutes later.

"We've all finished eating now, so why don't you come over."

I walked up to her table and the friend who she wanted so badly for me to meet was the woman I just met wearing the mink coat! There were some other single guys from the church who I knew, so as I joined them, I made sure to pay attention to all their moves. I already decided that this Leslie was for me.

Helen said she had been texting me all day to get me to come to the service, but because my number was changed, I never got her messages. Helen said she had been trying to get Leslie to come and meet me ever since she and I met on that date. So after not receiving the text messages that Helen sent me, Leslie and I still met! My prayer was heard!

Helen became instrumental in us getting together after that day and was determined to get it going. She knew that I played the guitar and that Leslie sang, so Helen said she was going to put a band together! We had fun emailing for a week or so making potential song lists and opening the lines of communication, but I still didn't have her number. After we gathered for the first time at Helen's house, I got Leslie's number and we started talking.

In my list of 50+ qualities, I also had a picture in my mind of a beautiful, sweet yet strong, petite blonde—she was an exact match. Those were seeds I planted in my mind years before. I believe you've got to ask for what you want. "Ask, and you shall receive" applies for so many things. Be sure they are healthy!

So, of course, before I prayed that day in early January, I knew what I wanted. The moment I met her, I sensed that she was the girl from the list and after just a few months of dating, I knew I was right. It was so easy for me because I knew what I wanted, and I knew what I didn't want. I had also met lots of people who weren't a match, but I said that prayer and had written it all down and visualized her. I believe in the power of creation, and the power that God gives us. I believe it's also about desire and being prepared ... I did my homework!

Courting Leslie was just great fun; it was scintillating just to be with her and we enjoyed each other's company. One snowy night, we were leaving Helen's house and I cleaned the snow off both of our cars. It was just a little thing, but she was thrilled and said nobody had ever done something like that for her before. She thought I was a decent guy and allowed me to call her and we started dating.

On our first 'real date' we went to an Amway meeting in Manhattan where I was presenting. I called and said, "Hey,

I'll be in Manhattan tonight for a meeting, wanna come?" She worked in Midtown, so it made it easy for her to say yes.

On our way home, we still talk about this today, we stopped at a diner for a bite to eat. During our conversation, Leslie mentioned she was interested in buying a car but the car she really wanted was too expensive. I asked her if she ever thought of a certified, pre-owned car from a reputable dealer, something with a warranty. She had never thought of it but was excited at the prospect of having the opportunity.

The next morning, I woke up early and got online. I found several cars that I thought she would like however, the one at the bottom of the list was one that just seemed right. I sent her the link and I said, "Hey, do you like white?" Within a week, she and her brother looked at it and that day she bought the car. That was kind of funny, but it showed her immediately that she could trust me to care about her.

While Leslie and I were getting to know one another, I would have an occasional session with Rachel, but much less often than any time in the past. I was very excited because I was sure I had met my life partner, so I wasn't really distracted by anything else. I was working diligently growing my business; I was focused on my son, as our lives were moving forward. There were struggles in the business, but I was kind of numb to those because of the excitement of the courtship. Rachel knew I was seeing Leslie, but she was surprised when I told her that I planned to propose; Rachel didn't know we were that serious but was extremely happy for Leslie and me.

"Do you ever think about forgiving that woman, Lou?" Rachel asked one evening when I had just stopped by to say hi and tell her my news.

"Yeah, I do, and it remains very prominent in my mind."

"Go on ..."

"Well ... after meeting Leslie, courting and finding love I

looked back and thought that was such a powerful moment in time. When I let the anger go and forgave that woman from my childhood, it enabled me to open myself to this beautiful new person in my life. Leslie is very different than any other woman I have ever known. She's just so very pure and very sweet."

"I wish you could see your face right now," said Rachel with a laugh. "Forgiveness has opened your **heart**. Now it's full of joy and happiness! Leslie would have never found her way in to your heart without that. When I first met you, Lou, you were filled with fear and terror. There was a great deal of anger and a lack of trust that was preventing you from living a healthy, free life.

"Yeah, I can see that now," I replied. "I really didn't trust too many people in my life. Once I started letting go and trusting more, better things started happening. Thinking about everything that we've done, I've learned that each person's journey towards healing is as individual as they are… I hesitated, we all need to find our own path."

"Very good, Lou!" she teased. I grinned, saying "I have come a long way and am feeling proud of myself."

"This has been your personal journey, Lou, but that doesn't mean other people can't go through similar steps. They can go through their own journey and use some of the same resources, right, but they have to pay attention to what's going on inside themselves to find the right steps for their path to a happier life … just like you have done."

24

Leslie was so very different from anyone else I had ever known, and soon after we fell in love, I planned to ask her to marry me. I fully accepted how powerful the prayer, meditating, and reading had been as well as all the work with on myself with Charles, Rachel and my other mentors. Yet my faith was always there with me; my faith along with my daily quiet time kept me going. I knew while going through so many problems that it was a test of my faith and will, but I just kept moving forward as I learned to let go.

As I've mentioned, before my healing began, I felt like I had to control every outcome, everything I said or did had to be perfect. Later, I learned that sometimes we can have any kind of plan we want, but we cannot always control the outcome. Also, the bigger lesson was that many times we must change or adjust the plan to achieve our desired outcome. This was the one I needed to learn!

I needed to be flexible, and as much as it might feel wrong, we must learn to know when to go with the flow at times. I had to learn to see what happened and then respond to that. If we are too controlling or rigid in our plans, when things go wrong, we get stressed, overwhelmed, and worn out.

I grew to understand that if signing up a new client didn't go exactly to plan; I had to trust both in God and in myself. I was beginning to trust that maybe God had a better plan … maybe my coach or mentor had a better idea. If I continued to work smartly and diligently, I became more confident that my company would grow, and we would find new clients. I had to trust my employees, my clients, and my suppliers then really believe that good things were going to happen to *me*. Because of my previous lack of trust, I tried to force these good things to happen, but once I learned to let go of trying to control too much, my life changed dramatically.

A key time for not over planning was when I felt it was time to talk to Leslie about my past and some of the challenges I faced. I wanted her to know who she was getting involved with; no negative surprises for her later. I decided to let things come out as necessary. It had been such a big deal in the past, but I had moved on significantly. This was the new me, she was becoming involved with.

As we started dating seriously, one of the first things that came up was discussing the prospect of having children together. She told me she could not have children. Not that she wouldn't, she physically couldn't have any. She simply stated that if this was an issue for me, then she was not the right woman. Because I had always wanted to have more children, that was initially a challenge, but I went home, and thought about it.

I already had a 15-year-old son and if I started having more children, I was concerned I would have less time for him. Louis had been through enough. I still wanted to pour more of my time into him, so I prayed about it and thought it through. I also realized I had a lot of business goals and thought how much time that would take away from everyone if we had more children. I accepted that if I wanted to marry Leslie, I wasn't going to have more children. I was fine with it and I told her so.

What's interesting is that once I decided to accept this outcome, I was free of worrying about starting a new family and the impact on Louis. Sometimes I still think about the idea of having children with Leslie and wish it could have happened, but I love my son and enjoy our ever-deepening relationship. I could have missed out on things with him if I started another family. Also, I get to be around our friends' children, so I can be silly and have fun with them, and that's great!

After that, we started having more heart to heart chats. My goal was to be authentic and honest, but I knew I didn't have to spill everything out in one sitting. It was a process. I began to fall in love with the process of life! We started talking about our mutual past a little bit at a time, touching on some of the things we experienced. She had been through a rough time with a guy who was abusive and had even threatened to kill her, but she finally got out of that unhealthy marriage. I told her that as a child I was abused, and I had been to a lot of different therapy sessions.

We didn't get into the detail of the abuse. She knew it was physical and sexual abuse, as well as some ritualistic abuse, but she came to understand enough to learn to trust me. She saw I was being honest. I think it helped bring us together because she saw into my heart; she saw I was open, she never questioned me about it beyond what I told her. We respected that bad things had happened to both of us and that we dealt with them. I was continuing to deal with my issues to let go of the old junk. I think she saw I was genuinely working to grow to be free of my past.

Occasionally we talk about it. When I have a session with Rachel, Leslie is there for me. She doesn't need to know details unless I choose to tell her, and that's okay for both of us.

Just after I met Leslie, things were turning around. My son and I were getting along great. He was happy and working hard in a private high school that I gratefully could afford. Everything was improving.

I continued with my daily routine of workouts and quiet time and spending time with my son, but I was reenergized and excited because I knew Leslie was the right woman. I was very happy, and people could tell right away when they saw me that something was going on. After only three months together, shortly after I shared my proposal plans with Rachel, I went to buy the ring.

"I'm looking for an engagement ring," I said to the owner of this old-fashioned jewelry shop in another neighborhood. "I'm kind of new at this; haven't done this in years!"

"Well, I have got one here," he replied and pulled a huge rock out of a display cabinet.

Not really liking the ring, I asked, "So how much is that?"

"I'll do it for $20,000 for you."

"Wow! I've been out of the market too long," I replied. "What else do you have?"

"Not much else right now, but I can make one for you." This clearly wasn't the right place for me, but it was a start!

Because things were going easier for me, like finding her car so quickly, I asked Wendy my trainer, where I could find a ring. She sent me to a local family run jewelry store named Braunschweiger Jewelers - www.braunschweiger.com. It's funny how life works sometimes; I had purchased from this store before but didn't think they would have anything I could afford. The manager was a lovely lady named Mary with an Irish brogue who has become a friend of ours. I went through my same, "I'm new to this," speech, and she showed me a couple of rings, and I said, "No, they are too gaudy."

"Wait, I have one right here, and it's unique," she said with a twinkle in her sweet Irish eyes, "it's one of a kind, an estate piece. I have no idea where it came from, but it's platinum with diamonds."

"I'll take it," I said the minute I set eyes on it. Within less than five minutes, I had this ring picked out.

"Well, that was easy!" I said.

"Well, that's how it's supposed to be," she replied. "Life shouldn't be so hard all the time, and things should be fun; life should be a little easier."

So, I put a deposit on the ring and life started to become a whirlwind and the excitement was building. I knew I was going to ask her to marry me, and things were going great. I took my son to a family vacation place we have, and when we were playing golf, I told him how serious I was with Leslie. His reply was simply, "No kidding Dad! Like everybody can tell!"

"Well, I just wanted you to be the first to know that she is very special to me."

"But it's so obvious Dad, and it's the same with her!"

I introduced her to my mom at Easter time before we were due to visit her parents in June. She came to my mom's house for dinner, and my mom's companion, an older gentleman we've known for years, started talking with Leslie. Within five minutes, they had worked out that his brother and sister-in-law were ministers at the church that she had been attending prior to us meeting at Liquid Church. Leslie knew and highly respected his brother. They started crying at the table because that minister had recently passed away. Yet another thing had just beautifully fallen into place with this amazing connection. All these positive reinforcements along the way were happening, and so we just kept going.

25

Believing in certain traditions, I wanted to speak to her dad to get his blessing before I proposed. We arranged a visit for early June 2012. This trip was combined with her brother, sister-in-law and their son who were also going to be there. Of course, the engagement was going to be a surprise for Leslie, so here again was a challenge in my new learning of flexibility.

With the airport's security measures, I didn't want to have the ring in my pocket, so I hid it in my carryon bag along with a couple of boxes of beautiful chocolates for her parents.

"Leslie, I need you to watch my bag; make sure no one touches it," I said as I was unloading the car that took us to the airport.

"Okay," she replied, giving me a strange look.

"I mean don't move and don't leave this bag alone, okay? You've got to have your eye on that bag at all times."

"What kind of chocolates are these? What else you got in there?"

"Oh, nothing. I have this thing about getting my bag stolen."

I got another look, but she seemed to accept I wasn't totally crazy. We got through security and boarded the plane. Every time I got up, I made sure the bag was there. When we got to her parents' house, they were out, so we decided to get a late lunch.

"I'm going to leave the bag at your parents' house; is that alright?"

She told me later she didn't say anything because she liked me. At the time, she had thought I was uptight because of how I was acting over some chocolates! I left the bag at her parents' house because I figured it was safer than the hotel where I was going to stay.

The next morning, Leslie and her mom were going to a funeral for a family friend and suggested that I could go over to her parent's house to meet her dad and get to know him. Excellent! I had this notion that I would have some time to talk with her dad and ask him for his daughter's hand in marriage. This was a perfect plan or, so I thought.

As I was pulling into the driveway around the agreed time for my arrival, I saw a car with an out of state license plate and realized her brother and family were already there. He and his wife and son had arrived about four hours earlier than expected! Now my time for speaking with her dad alone was already in jeopardy. "Great!" I thought. "When am I going to be able to talk to her dad?"

This was such a test for me, not only to find the opportunity to ask the question, but to remain calm and think on my feet when things didn't go according to plan. I wanted everything to be perfect and this was the first of many events that didn't go as planned. I later realized the entire trip was turning out to be a real journey of faith and courage for me. The only known things were that I had the ring; I was going to ask Leslie to marry me and I was going to ask her dad's permission first. That's all I knew.

Before I had a moment to talk to him alone, it was already lunchtime and Leslie and her mom walked in the door. We had planned to go out later in the afternoon to a food festival and that's where I figured I'd pop the question. I thought to myself, "how am I going to ask her dad before we leave when there's a house full of people?" So, I said a little prayer.

"Alright Lord give me a break here. I really need a break..." and as soon as I said that, her dad stood up and walked down the stairs of their split-level home, announcing he was going out to bring in the trash cans.

"I'll come and help," I said, feeling like an eight-year-old.

"Oh, I'm fine; I can handle it, you know," he replied over his shoulder and I dread to think what his face looked like or what he thought about the guy his daughter had brought home.

Still, I ran out after him and got him to sit at a small table on their front patio, saying I just wanted to talk to him. Before I could say any more, her nephew came out and sat down with us! By now, I was sweating like I was in a sauna. In my head, I was starting to think; "Get out of here kid!" Then Leslie and her mom came out to see what we were doing! I really was being tested! But they eventually took her nephew inside. Finally, her dad and I had a few minutes to speak alone!

"I have been trying to ask you all morning; I know I don't know you well and you don't know me, but I wanted to ask you for your daughter's hand in marriage."

He looked like it wasn't that much of a surprise, but his face stayed serious.

"Well ... I just want you to know that I don't want her around anybody too controlling. She has had that happen to her before."

"I understand, and I promise you she can be herself. That's why I love her and want to marry her."

After some more heart to heart talk, he said, "It's okay with me, but I'm not the boss. You'll have to ask her mother."

I thought, "no way, Lord!" I did what I came here to do. With her dad happy, I was all set with the ring in my pocket, along with a card that had a little girl with a veil on the front. Inside, I wrote, 'Will you marry me?' At the bottom, I put a 'yes' and a 'no', with an instruction underneath to circle her desired answer. In parenthesis, I wrote, 'Please circle yes!' She was already accustomed to receiving cards from me, so I thought that if she found it, I would just say I was going to send it to her later. To this day, I frequently give her cards.

We went downtown to the Old Market area of Omaha, with its cobblestone streets and many nice shops, then headed out to the river and the park. The expected food and wine festival ended up being a beer and barbecue festival, so it wasn't what I would have chosen, but it was going to have to do. Again, not my picture-perfect plan, but I remained flexible and on a mission. All I had to do now was to find a nice romantic spot to pop that all-important, life-changing question.

We got something to eat, met some folks she knew and walked around some more, but I just couldn't find the right spot and I started getting frustrated. The old me would have been panicking by now, but I told myself to chill and enjoy the moment. As soon as I did that, I saw this beautiful spot, a boardwalk that led out to a big deck overlooking the river. It was perfect, but then two older women turned up and it was clear they weren't going to leave!

So, we started walking again and I just couldn't find the right place; then we came to a gate that seemed locked.

"It's open … are you okay?" Leslie said as she reached around and flipped the latch open. I simply smiled and tried to hide my frustration.

We continued to walk and I started to mumble that I couldn't find a place and eventually came upon a path that led to a lush green area—as we got nearer, I realized that it had goose droppings all over it and that the grass was very wet. As I started to complain a bit, Leslie just put her hand on my arm.

"How about we sit on that nice park bench?" she said gently.

Perfect! I was sure I was about to explode with the stress, but as we sat down, I was simply so excited again. After chatting for just a few moments, I pulled out the card.

"I was going to mail this to you, but I want you to have it now," I said as I was digging in my pocket for the ring.

As she opened the card, I got down on one knee. She looked at the card and looked at me and I said, "Will you marry me?"

"Are you sure?" she replied. I almost laughed. If she knew what

I had gone through to get the ring here, speak to her dad and then to find the right spot.

"Of course, I'm sure!" I said with a grin, then my expression turned serious again. "But are you?"

"Yes!" she exclaimed, and my heart did somersaults. I did it!

I was so incredibly happy and we had such an exciting time. We both had fake tattoos done on our arms. We were going to try to trick her mom into looking at the tattoo while Leslie was pointing with her ring finger.

"Hey Mom, look at my tattoo!" she said back at the house.

"Yeah, honey," her mom replied, not really paying attention.

"Mom, I got a tattoo! Look at my tattoo, Mom!"

"Yeah, very nice Leslie."

"Mom!"

But still her mom didn't look. By now, there were probably a dozen people at the house, her nieces and a couple of neighbors as well. It was the woman from next door that suddenly screeched in her mom's ear.

"Hey! What?" asked her mom, looking around.

"I got engaged, Mom!" shouted Leslie.

We had a big celebration and I finally started to relax, just enjoying the moment. It had been a very wild ride because I went totally on faith. Despite my frustrations, I knew her dad would be okay with the marriage and that we would form a friendship; I knew it would be fine. Yes, I had done some planning, but doing it on the fly like that was totally out of character and secretly, I was very proud of myself.

The other part of the story is that we decided to stay celibate the entire time we dated until we married. That was important for me because it was (still is) a very healthy way to have a relationship. Today, it doesn't go with everybody's thoughts, but it worked for us. I realized how many emotional ties I had with those unhealthy relationships from my past and I wanted this one to remain as pure and healthy as it had started out.

One morning shortly afterwards, I was walking back to my car from a client meeting and reflected on that decision to wait to be truly intimate with one another. The decision was made when I was working with Charles and Rachel. I admitted my mistakes and forgave that woman who had been with my uncle. I still can't explain how this all worked to come together, yet I know I have been set free because I was willing to be humble and honest to admit some things about and accept my past.

All of this was very spiritual for me. I found that once I forgave that unknown woman, let her go, established my own healthy habits with new beliefs, I had the strength and respect not to have premarital sex. I just thought it would be a better way to see if I could think clearly and not let the sex interfere with our thought processes. It really helped us have a solid relationship— then and now. This is something very powerful that society doesn't accept. There really is a blessing on this type of relationship. Because we behaved 'differently' by staying pure, we have something so much stronger, a relationship so special and precious. It was all very foreign to me and my past.

26

The engagement was *such* an exciting time and as soon as we got home, we started planning the wedding, which was another faith journey; we planned to elope a long distance from New Jersey.

The years I served as a full-time Sheriff's Officer were spent in Eagle County, Colorado, living and working there was wonderful. During the 1970's and 1980's, prior to working at the Sheriff's Office, I spent much time staying with cousins who live in this magnificent valley. I purchased my own property in 1986. I grew to love the area and the majestic mountain views.

In the late 80's, a chapel was built in Beaver Creek at the base of the ski mountain. I had visited this wonderful place numerous times throughout the 1990's and into 2000's. After the divorce, when I wondered if I would marry again, I wanted it to take place in that beautiful location in Colorado. The Chapel at Beaver Creek www.beavercreekchapel.com was only recently built, with its stone walls, slate roof, and bell tower, it looks much older. Its setting, among the trees and enchanting gardens, is just perfect for a romantic wedding. Later, we met the builder of the chapel and found him and his wife to be loving and generous people. If you can get there, I highly recommend a visit.

Before meeting Leslie, I described these dreams in my journal and visualized a celebration dinner for hitting a big business goal, with some family members, some friends, and my soon-to-be bride. In my journal, I described how I would announce our engagement and ask Brad, my mentor who is a trained ordained minister and pastor to be the celebrant for our ceremony. Several parts of that dream have come true! The business goal was in the works, but while the engagement announcement part was different, Brad was our celebrant, and his wife, Shan, was our witness for our wedding in that spectacular and romantic chapel in Beaver Creek.

Learning to trust was also a big step for Leslie. After I described the chapel to her, without ever visiting, she agreed to be married there and planned the entire event long distance. It was only a very small affair. Our families were spread across the country and due to health situations limiting travel in our families, we didn't want to leave anyone out, so we agreed that we would elope and hold a celebration later.

This was a tough decision for us because, we wanted to share our special day with all our family and friends. Neither her dad or my mom's companion could travel. My son offered to be our photographer, which was a great idea! After some serious thought, we decided it would be best for everyone if we had a private, intimate wedding with just the two of us.

As our wedding day drew near, the excitement built because we worked out how special we wanted to make our ceremony. Leslie planned to sing a song as she walked down the aisle and I would play the guitar. She chose "Songbird" by Fleetwood Mac. While I initially protested saying it was written for the piano, I learned it and played it on my 12-string guitar. Unbeknownst to her, I found a meaningful piece from a songwriter in Nashville to surprise her midway through our ceremony. I practiced whenever I could. For me, this song was a way of sharing my love with Leslie on our special day.

On December 1st just 30 days prior to our wedding, Leslie's father passed away. This was so tough for her. I suggested we move the date, but she decided it was best to continue as planned; it was what her dad would have wanted. I gave her much credit for her strength in that emotional time. Deep down, we both wished our moms could be with us, but she knew her mom was not ready to travel. My mom wanted so much to be there but graciously understood the situation and felt it wouldn't be right to attend without Leslie's mom there too.

During our setup, the caretaker, a lovely and caring woman who helped organize the location, mentioned the chapel had Wi-Fi. In a flash of inspiration, we decided to have our moms present via FaceTime! We set up our respective phones, checked the connection, and set them on a music stand facing the altar where we would stand throughout the ceremony.

After he agreed to perform the wedding for us, I told Brad I wanted us to write our own vows. I knew him for close to 20 years and was sure he would understand. He was the one who had introduced me to Charles and gave credibility to the healing work Charles and I were doing. We discussed the vows for a while, and he eventually told me that he felt that the vows I wanted seemed more like a business agreement, they didn't have the depth of the biblical marriage vows he would want us to take.

Knowing him, as long as I had, and assured of his solid values, I let go of having to control this part of the ceremony; I knew that he only had our best interests in mind. I agreed that he could handle the vows after he had explained the spiritual importance of how these were designed in God's word. He asked me to trust him in this. There was that word again… "trust".

With FaceTime connections established, the ceremony he developed—based on *Faith*, *Hope*, and *Love*—was just beautiful. This was not just a typical or canned scripture verse, but a deep and meaningful discourse on each of those three words and how they would apply to our lives, intertwined with God, family, and friends going forward.

At the pre-agreed moment, Brad gave me the signal, I looked at Leslie and I told her I had a surprise for her. I picked up my guitar then sang a song for her: "Here We Stand" by Tony Carter. Our eyes were locked throughout the entire time, I felt how intense her focus was on me. I also sensed Brad and Shan watching me as I sang in adoration of my new bride.

After I finished, during some of his preaching, I teased Brad by asking if I could now kiss her, but he just stayed on track and continued to make it a powerful ceremony. Then I was finally told I could kiss my bride—what a wonderful moment that was. To have come from those times of the depths of despair before I went to Oklahoma, to this moment of pure joy was something I knew would happen but the joy I felt was more intense than I ever imagined.

The entire ceremony was spirit filled. Our love was felt by everyone; our moms, Brad and Shan, as well as the caretaker, videographer and photographer. The last three spoke to us separately. Each of them told us they had never experienced so much love in a ceremony before and expressed how happy they were for us and to have been there to witness it.

After our brief honeymoon in Colorado, I was on my way to my office on the first day back to work. I started thinking about all the recent months and how much my life had changed. Along with my long-term belief in God, I now believed in myself. This was such an important part of the whole faith thing. I was now seeing and believed, that good things would happen for me, which the 'old me' just couldn't fathom. Life was supposed to be good and it was meant to be full of joy and cherished. And it was.

27

When I was 12 I started working at my grandfather's store along with my dad and his brother. Eventually, my father opened his business across the street, which is when I began helping him. Because the stores were so close to each other, we would visit often and provide help and support. From the 1970's through the 1990's my dad owned and operated a successful retail store with two locations where we sold and serviced business machines. Being prior to computers, we sold typewriters, calculators, copiers, facsimile machines and the like. Thinking back, this may have influenced my career decisions.

One day in the late 80's, my grandfather was in my dad's office and in the middle of the conversation, he just stopped talking. We weren't sure what was happening so we called 911 and got him to the hospital. Eventually, we learned that he had a stroke and had to stay in hospital for quite a while.

Not too long after that incident, I was away in New York State camping in a cabin with some buddies. One night out in those quiet woods, I had a dream. In it, I distinctly remember my grandfather lying on a hospital bed and saying, "I'm waiting to see you, so I can die."

I was a bit shaken when I woke. I knew I needed to go see him. The dream was so powerful that I went home and told my dad that I needed to see my grandfather, so he took me. I went to spend time with him, although he couldn't verbally communicate, he acknowledged I was there. I told him I love him and sat for a while, being there but not sure of how or what to feel. Within a week of that visit, he passed away. At the time, I was still young and naïve, and I thought that was weird but knew there was a connection. Then the same type of thing happened with my uncle.

In April of 2015, I was in negotiations to sell my company, dealing with the sale of our old home, and purchasing and remodeling a new one. We were renting back our old home for thirty days while waiting for the remodel to finish. When we found out the project was greatly delayed and could not stay any longer in our place, we organized the moving company to move our belongings but not us. The builder said it would be just a couple more weeks, so we reached out to some wonderful friends who graciously offered that we could temporarily move in with them.

Six weeks later, we called the builder and told him we were moving in no matter what. I was not very cordial or patient and was ready to fight to get this completed. The stress of this, along with all that was happening with the sale of my business, was immense. I started to feel I was getting angry again, and not just at the builder, so I called Rachel.

I really thought I was finished with all the issues I had been holding against my uncle and my grandmother. We had many sessions, each one like peeling back the layers of an onion. I would go deeper into my spirit and forgive. Then I would go further and further into my subconscious. In the beginning, it had been more about me letting go of the anger against him and getting that out and saying what I had to say to him. Then I said I forgave him and did. Somehow, even though I participated at 100% during these sessions I went as deep as I could. Yet when I went back in again and worked with Rachel on this new session, I realized that I was *still* holding onto something, somewhere at an even deeper level inside.

I had two more sessions with her. In the first one, I found I was still very angry with my grandmother for something that happened with the abuse. I let it all out. I was mad at her and let her know it. Finally, I let that go and thought okay, "I am finally done here." Then something else came up, and I was anxious once again.

"Something is going on and bothering me, but I can't put my finger on it," I told Rachel, and we agreed another session."

This was very deep in my subconscious where I was still holding something against my uncle. This time, just like the years of sessions I had, I thought; "Well, just let him have it! Give it to him good!" I was angry and yelling and cursing at him for all his wrongdoing until I realized I was now well and truly finished with him. I don't recall our exact conversation, but I ended up saying again that I forgave him and truly let him and all the negative emotions towards him go. I wanted him out of my life.

"I forgive you. I set you free to go wherever you need to go. I love you. I send you on your way. I totally forgive you."

Yes, I forgave him again. This time was different. This time I also told him I *loved* him. For me forgiveness comes from love. I truly meant it. On this deep level, I had learned to love the person. I did not condone what he did, I just let it go. I was finally over all of what happened with him in the past. I accepted that from a deep spiritual level I could love someone who hurt me so severely. What was powerful was in some way, it felt like I had been directly connected to him despite forgiving him all those times before. A few weeks later, I received a phone call from a family member who told me that my uncle had just passed away.

I was quite surprised because I didn't know he was ill. I knew he had financial struggles over the years and was living in a room at a boarding house, but this coming so soon after that last session? Did my forgiveness one more time and that declaration of love finally allow him to go? Was he hanging on like my grandfather to say goodbye or maybe ask for forgiveness? Did he know how to ask for it? Had he not really believed that I forgave him the first time? Too many questions flooded into my head for me to even try to understand the depth of forgiveness and the power of love ... but this power can never be denied.

I decided I would attend the wake, a typical Catholic event held in a funeral parlor. The body had been embalmed, dressed nicely, and laid out in an open casket to have people come say their goodbyes and see him one final time.

There were very few people at the wake, maybe 25 in total which surprised me as we came from a very large family. My grandmother alone had 13 siblings. Of course, most of them had passed away, but they had multiple children who were close to her. In attendance was one of my grandmother's nieces, several cousins along with one of my sisters who came to show support and pay their respects.

As I looked around, I realized that most of the men were still dressed like they did back in the 1970's—black leather jackets and black shirts opened enough to show their chest adorned with gold neck chains. I was the only one dressed in a suit and tie. I was a bit surprised because many of the attendees looked much older than they were. But I didn't care about that; I was there for myself. I just wanted to know that I could go and be at peace with seeing this man again. Even though he was dead, I wanted to prove to myself that I was truly over all that happened and that I was no longer holding onto any ill will towards him.

In the Catholic tradition, I knelt next to the casket and said a prayer.

"Lord, I have already forgiven him." I looked at my uncle once again and said, "I forgive you," as I thought in my heart, "Lord you can forgive him, too."

I stood up and had no emotions towards him. I was now at peace. You may call this closure, but for me it was also a test to see how I was going to react to seeing him. Nothing! What stunned me the most was that I didn't even recognize him. If I had seen him walking down the street, I would not have known who he was. I grew up with this man, my father's brother. He abused me for years, and he was in our family life constantly until I was in my early twenties and moved away. I thought I would at least recognize his face, but no.

I offered my condolences to his son and some other family members. Then I left, driving through the town where we all grew up. I traveled along that long main street with many familiar sights and then passed the locations where both family businesses I worked in and grew up around were located. I realized that both of those buildings were now gone. The building my father owned then sold had been torn down to add much-needed parking for a large grocery store. The other location was the one my grandfather started all those years ago in 1942. It thrived for many decades then my uncle took it over—after a few years of his ownership, it had been burned to the ground leaving only an empty grass lot.

With all the memories that place brought back, it struck me that the abuse from my uncle drove me away from that town. As a child, and into my teen years, I deeply yearned for freedom. I knew I had to get away from this place. I really didn't know why until that moment when it came through loud and clear. Had all those heinous events not happened to me, maybe, just maybe, I might have stayed and become just like everyone else at that funeral.

I was overcome with mixed emotions as I drove away that day. I was raised loving that town. Publicly my family was well known and respected. I grew up with many school friends and much of our family continued to live there even after we moved away. Now I didn't want anything to with it. I realized that the abuse and all the situations I had found myself in were really a gift. Yes, a gift! It may sound very odd to say that, but it's how I felt that day and still do today.

That 'gift' got me away from there, so I could grow to become who I wanted to be and live the life I wanted to live. To break free of the emotional ties that bound me. To have the chance to live up to my potential. That was an incredibly powerful moment in my life. I realized I had *truly* released *all* those negative emotions! I felt so very grateful.

Things were very different now. I was able to have a better relationship with my family. I was able to have a better relationship with God. I was able to love myself. There was much more love in my life! It was the forgiveness that allowed the loving. The more I forgave, the more I was able to love, and the more I had the capacity to love people. The more I loved, the more I had the capacity to forgive. They are both intertwined together. I had forgiven those who hurt me. That to me is to truly love someone.

In addition, I forgave myself for holding on to those things for so long, for feeling bad that those things happened, for any guilt or any shame or even feeling responsible for those things. Now all that was gone too, and I knew that all the dark parts of my life were truly over.

People hurt each other. Whether it's done intentionally or unintentionally, we hurt one another. What you do with that hurt and what you do with that pain is largely going to determine the outlook of your life. So many people go through life bitter, angry, resentful, and, well the list could go on, but all those negative emotions or feelings will cause more problems than the original act which made us feel bad. Forgiveness is the act of releasing the desire to retaliate, hurt or punish someone—or yourself—for an offense. It's an act of grace and is never something you can force or pretend. There are no shortcuts and there are certainly no half-measures.

As I did, you must feel the resentment, bitterness, hurt, or anger before you can begin to forgive. Don't let yourself be wrapped up in the idea of revenge. Thoughts of getting even when someone does you wrong come to all of us at some time, but revenge reduces you to your worst self. It puts you on the same level with those hurtful people we claim to abhor. Revenge also makes *YOU* the victim. It says I have no control over my thoughts and feelings and allows someone else to control you. As difficult as it is, remember, let it go.

To thrive as individuals, we must resist this predictable lust for revenge and seek to right wrongs more positively. Revenge might make you feel good in the short-term, but it's still a negative solution. Forgiveness can only ever make you feel good and more positive about yourself. The act of forgiving will improve your health, your relationships, your overall life.

You may not need to go as deep as I did. It may only be a simple prayer or sincere phone call to take the high road and say, "Remember that time when ...? Well, it hurt me and I've carried it around for a while, but now I want you to know that I forgive you." Once you've done that, just wait and let the other person respond before hanging up. I'm not saying that this is easy, it's not. The relationship, however, can truly heal...You'll be amazed at the results!

It might be done in email or a text and you can still do it if the person is no longer living. You can still go through the motions of writing a letter or have a conversation with them in your mind like I did. Once you really mean it, your life will change ... honestly.

As I've learned for myself, the healing process of recovering from such as abuse requires enormous compassion for *yourself* as you get started on the journey of self-inquiry and recovery. It necessitates looking at the situation and asking: "What kind of brokenness and suffering could ever make a person want to commit such grievous harm?"

You're not excusing the behavior or returning to it but grasping how emotionally crippled the abuser is. Think about my experiences with that woman, and how much later in her life she was still tormented by her past actions. Forgiveness is a huge step to take, but it's the path to freedom.

Forgiveness is a life altering, paradigm-shifting solution for transforming bitterness, hurt, anger, resentment and many more negative feelings. It frees you from the trap of short-term revenge so you can experience life more fully with much greater happiness and confidence, better relationships, and even better finances. It has for me!

I've learned that Christ came to forgive so we could have a true relationship with God. To be forgiven yourself, I encourage you to ask Christ to come into your heart and free you from your sin. If you sincerely ask Him in, He will enter your heart, and you will start a new journey in your life as I have.

Forgiveness does more for *you* than anyone else could. It liberates you from negativity and lets you move forward in your life to create bigger and better things. Forgiving won't change the past, but it will give you the freedom of knowing you are so much more than what you thought or felt you were.

May God continue to bless you on your journey.

EPILOGUE

There are so many corollaries here, so many parallels to the forgiveness; going into my subconscious mind, letting go of negative emotions, and my health quickly improving. Over and over, I saw that my beliefs were changing and my life was improving.

Until I hit that low spot in my life; getting fired while my marriage was in a terrible mess, I didn't even know why I felt so bad, so insecure, and so lacking in self-respect. Something had to change. So, I started asking questions. This began with self-inquiry. I was reluctant at first, to admit I needed help. Once I allowed Brad, Charles, Rachel and others, into my life, I started to improve. If you have issues in your life, start asking questions. Ask yourself: "Why do I feel like this?" "What is the truth here?" "What is the reason this is bothering me?" There are always reasons and always good people to ask for help. Be patient and listen for the answers. If you are sincere you will receive answers. It may take some time, so press on. Then you can start yourself on a better road.

Something else I came to understand was, many of my relationships were too emotionally tied, almost codependent. Typically, I was the most emotionally involved. I would get so drawn in by people's drama and their life that I would want to help save them. I would be sucked in by men, women, couples, it didn't matter who. I was just drawn into their problems, which seemed to suck the life and energy right out of me. These were my friends, I loved them, and I would do anything for them. However, if I did want the patience, empathy, and energy to help them, I had to learn to take care of myself first. Later I discovered these types of relationships didn't serve anyone. I was feeling like the hero but, it was unhealthy. If you are in a codependent relationship it hurts everyone involved. Find a way to get help. Start by reading the book: *Codependent No More* by Melody Beattie.

In those early days after what I've referred to in this book as my downfall, my emotions were raw. I wasn't experiencing real inner peace. Therefore, I was always looking somewhere outside myself for that peace, for that satisfaction, for that love. I looked anywhere and everywhere except where it all comes from: meeting God inside myself. I learned that my quiet prayer, meditation, and reading sessions were time building a stronger relationship with God. Time alone with just Him brought me closer to Him and who I am. I would nurture myself, which also brought me to a deeper sense of self and connection with God. Of course, times with others are also helpful, but I found that without my base of 'alone time', those other experiences weren't as fruitful or fulfilling.

As I became emotionally and spiritually healthier, I found I didn't really need anybody to help me feel good about myself. I am now okay with me! What a relief!! I have God, I have myself, Leslie and Louis; that's really all I need. Of course, I want companionship, friendship and fellowship, but now my relationships have changed for the better. They are based on common values and interests not need. Unhealthy people are no longer in my inner circle. Some of the unhealthy people just disappeared naturally, and for others, I had to say goodbye. Most of the changes happened intuitively as I grew. I used to talk to many of my friends a few times a week or a month, but when I stopped calling, I simply didn't hear from them anymore. It had all come from me. They weren't really my friends, or I wasn't important in their lives, but I had felt like I wanted to be— needed to be. I was inserting myself into people's lives because

I wanted to be their friend, so I could get the acceptance and even some recognition that I didn't get as a child.

I realized how emotionally demanding it had been because I was the one always running around. I thought everybody loved me because I was constantly giving and loving, but many were just being polite and didn't really care at all. When I got busy focusing on my life, I started to get healthy and things changed for the better.

One final note, in May 2015, we were getting ready to move into a new home. While emptying my desk, I found that notebook with the 52 qualities and showed Leslie. I said, "See, you are right here on these pages!" She was blown away as she had never believed me. But then she teased me—and still does—that I had been a little over-zealous!!

I encourage you to start on the road to emotional freedom. It is a journey. One in which you will need immense love and patience! To help you I've added a list of resources that have helped me and many others. Know that this is only a very small list of hundreds and hundreds of books I've read, studied and applied. Yeah it took time! It was time well invested.

Feel free to reach out to me at Lou@LouSamara.com if you want some encouragement or maybe a book recommendation.

Remember you can break out of anything you are facing. You may have some thoughts like; "*it isn't possible*", "*it isn't worth it*" or "*I can't face it*", "*I'm not that type of person*", "*it's too hard*", "*it hurts too much*", "*I'm too old*", "*I don't care*", "*I don't need help*"...These and thoughts or statements like these are all lies designed to protect your ego. Remember until you get these lies under control you will live in bondage. Your mind is more powerful than you realize. Remember, you are not your mind. You, control your mind. Jump in with an open mind and ask lots of questions until to get to the bottom of your situation.

I hope the resources here set you on a path that brings you true emotional freedom. You can find these and others on my website at: www.forgivenesseffect.com

Thank you again for taking the time to read this book.

May God bless you on your journey.

Lou Samara

To take advantage of a Free Offer go to:
www.forgivenesseffect.com/freeoffer

RESOURCES

The following is a list of resources that have benefited me and, I hope they can help and serve you on your journey.

Books:

I use the NIV Life Application Study Bible and Message Bible. Both are easy to read and understand. I've found Zondervan a reliable source for Christian Based Books and Bibles: http://www.zondervan.com

Think and Grow Rich
Outwitting the Devil
Your Right to Be Rich
Napoleon Hill – www.naphill.org

How to Win Friends and Influence People
How to Stop Worrying and Start Living
Dale Carnegie - https://www.dalecarnegie.com

The Magic of Thinking Big
Dr. David Schwartz

Stop Walking on Eggshells
Paul Mason and Randi Kreger

The Power of Positive Thinking
Dr. Norman Vincent Peale

The Success Principles
Jack Canfield - http://jackcanfield.com

Wisdom for Winners
The Ultimate Gift
Jim Stovall - http://www.jimstovall.com

Positive Personality Profiles
Dr. Robert A. Rohm - www.personalityinsights.com

Failing Forward
John C. Maxwell - https://www.johnmaxwell.com

Seven Choices for Success and Significance
How to Get Anything You Want
Stairway to Success
Nido Qubein - http://www.nidoqubein.com
www.highpoint.edu

Boundaries
Henry Cloud and John Townsend - www.boundariesbooks.com

The Journey
Brandon Bays - https://www.thejourney.com

Who Switched Off My Brain
Switch on Your Brain
Dr. Caroline Leaf - https://drleaf.com

Victory over the Darkness
The Bondage Breaker
Neil T. Anderson - ficm.org

Codependent No More
Melody Beattie - melodybeattie.com

The Sedona Method
Hale Dwoskin - https://www.sedona.com

Rich Dad Poor Dad
Cash Flow Quadrant
Robert Kiyosaki - https://www.richdad.com

Seeds of Greatness
Dr. Denis Waitley - http://deniswaitley.com

Modalities And Websites:

Rachel Linnett
May those who are ready and ripe for healing make contact with me, so I can assist them on their journey towards freedom.
https://www.rachellinnett.com

Theophostic Prayer Ministry now called
Transformation Prayer Ministry
http://www.transformationprayer.org

Time Line Therapy
http://www.timelinetherapy.com

Gestalt Therapy
https://en.wikipedia.org/wiki/Gestalt_therapy

Neuro-Linguistic Programming
http://www.nlp.com/what-is-nlp

Acupuncture Association
http://www.asacu.org/state-organizations

Chiropractic Association
https://www.acatoday.org

Preventive Health Care Practitioner
Dr. Mark Bartiss - https://icamnj.com
Institute for Complementary and Alternative Medicine

For your area look here:
American College of Preventive Medicine
https://www.acpm.org

International Association of Reiki Professionals
https://iarp.org

Health Benefits of Forgiveness:
https://www.medicaldaily.com/how-forgiveness-benefits-your-health-forgiving-wrongdoers-can-expand-physical-fitness-316902

According to the Mayo Clinic, forgiveness brings with it plenty of health benefits, including improved relationships, decreased anxiety and stress, lower blood pressure, a lowered risk of depression, and stronger immune and heart health. Letting go of negative emotions can often have a remarkable impact on the body. Jan 7, 2015

For a Free Offer go to: www.forgivenesseffect.com/freeoffer

Personality
INSIGHTS
PRESS